The
Green
Witch's
GARDEN

Your Complete Guide to
CREATING AND CULTIVATING
A MAGICAL GARDEN SPACE

ARIN MURPHY-HISCOCK
AUTHOR OF *The Green Witch*

ADAMS MEDIA
NEW YORK LONDON TORONTO SYDNEY NEW DELHI

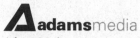

Adams Media
An Imprint of Simon & Schuster, Inc.
100 Technology Center Drive
Stoughton, Massachusetts 02072

Copyright © 2021 by Simon & Schuster, Inc.

First Adams Media hardcover edition December 2021

ADAMS MEDIA and colophon are trademarks of Simon & Schuster.

For information about special discounts for bulk purchases, please contact Simon & Schuster Special Sales at 1-866-506-1949 or business@simonandschuster.com.

The Simon & Schuster Speakers Bureau can bring authors to your live event. For more information or to book an event contact the Simon & Schuster Speakers Bureau at 1-866-248-3049 or visit our website at www.simonspeakers.com.

Interior design by Colleen Cunningham
Interior illustrations by Sara Richard
Interior images © 123RF/Eleonora Konnova; Getty Images/Boonyachoat, littleclie, Maksim-Manekin

Manufactured in the United States of America

3 2022

Library of Congress Cataloging-in-Publication Data has been applied for.

ISBN 978-1-5072-1587-6
ISBN 978-1-5072-1588-3 (ebook)

Dedication

This is for Ron, because, let's face it, you're the green thumb
in the family, and this green witch would be sad without you.
Thank you for our pretty gardens and for being patient when
I send you to the greenhouse with a very specific list.

Acknowledgments

As always, Ceri and Megan kept me sane during the writing process
of this book. I would be a sobbing mess without them. Being writers
as well, they know the trials of making a book into something that
can be read coherently. They also shored up my confidence when
I regularly wailed, "I have a black thumb, why am I writing this!"

Our garden tends to be a home for leftover plants, and I thank
Megan for that particularly; she inevitably has too much success starting tomato seedlings. She is also always happy to go to the greenhouse
with me and walk around looking at different varieties of everything;
we enable one another delightfully. The houseplants I bought on
our last trip are still alive, ten months later! (Allow me to knock on
wood.)

I would also be remiss if I did not publicly thank Brett Palana-
Shanahan, who has been a solid and supportive editor throughout the
majority of my career in various ways. She makes my work better, and
my books would all be the poorer without her guidance and suggestions. Thank you, Brett!

Contents

Introduction 9
How to Use This Book 10

Chapter 1
Green Witchcraft in the Garden • 11

Why You Need a Garden for Your Craft 12
Your Garden As a Spiritual Reflection of You 14
Building Your Connection to Nature 16
Recognizing the Natural Cycle 16
Working with Plant Spirits 19
Eco-Awareness 21
Regenerative Gardening 23
Alternative Gardens 26

Chapter 2
Magical Goals for Your Garden • 29

How Will You Use Your Garden? 30
Modifying an Existing Garden 34
A Garden for Cooking and Food 35
A Garden to Grow Magical Elements 37
A Magical Oasis Garden 38
Rewilding 40

Chapter 3

Kinds of Witch Gardens • 41

Basic Components of a Green Witch Garden 42

Astrological Gardens. 43

Moon Gardens 50

Elemental Gardens 57

Chapter 4

Plant Your Witch's Garden • 61

Indoors, Outdoors: What and Where 62

Indoors and Houseplants 62

Alternative Indoor Gardens. 67

Winter Gardening. 74

Vegetables from Kitchen Waste. 74

Windowsill and Window Box Gardens 76

Container Gardening 79

Outdoor Gardens 81

Chapter 5

Prepare Your Sacred Space • 83

Gather Your Tools. 84

Cleansing Your Garden Space 91

Bless Your Garden. 93

Choose Your Planting Cycle and Design 95

Create Your Garden Journal 96

Creating Records for Herbal Entries 100

Planning for Next Year's Garden. 104

Chapter 6

Choose What to Plant • 105

Plant What You Like. 106

Flowers 107

Herbs 121

Fruit 134

Vegetables 135

Trees 138

Mushrooms and Fungi 142

Ground Cover and Grains. 144

Chapter 7

Magic for a Healthy Garden • 149

Charms for Tools and Equipment. 150

Magic for Garden Protection and Health 152

Garden Health 158

Deities and Spirits Associated with Gardens 162

Garden Folklore and Traditions 163

Magical Tips for Caring for Your Garden 164

Amplifying the Magic of Your Ingredients 169

Adding Magical Decor to Your Garden. 170

Chapter 8

Make Magic with Your Harvest • 173

Cooking with Produce from Your Garden. 174

Divination with Your Garden 183

Using What You've Grown in Witchcraft 186

Chapter 9
Practice Witchcraft in the Garden • 193

Magic in Your Garden. 194

Drawing Magical Energy from the Garden. 196

Seasonal Celebrations in Your Garden. 199

Casting Spells in Your Garden 207

Using Your Garden for Meditation 211

In Conclusion 214

Bibliography 215

Hardiness Zones 217

Index. 219

Introduction

THE WAY OF THE GREEN WITCH is the path of the naturalist, the herbalist, and the healer. As a green witch you work closely with nature and its gifts and strive to build a relationship with the natural world. The act of working hands-on in a garden offers you a deep, rich, and personal connection with the life cycle of plants, which benefits both you and your practice.

For the green witch seeking to have a hand in curating their spiritual interaction with plants literally from the ground up, *The Green Witch's Garden* provides a basic introduction to gardening while also offering a cross-section of gardening lore, folk traditions, and magic. Inside you'll find information about planning your garden (either inside or out), suggestions for what plants may be beneficial, and ways to use your harvest in your magical practice.

Perhaps you haven't had the opportunity or inclination to work with living plants before. It's possible that your only interaction has been with plants in their harvested forms, either fresh or dried. If you haven't had the chance to work with green growing things in various stages from seed to plant, this book will help you think about how you can approach it. If you have worked with plants before, perhaps you haven't approached them from a spiritual direction, and this book can show you how.

You'll find that the experience of interacting with the energy of plants at different points of the life cycle is valuable for you as a green witch. For example, knowing how a seedling differs from a well-established plant gives you insight. Also, observing how the energy of a plant changes as it develops can help you examine ways to use those energies differently and further your practice.

Designed to support a green witch's exploration of creating a garden in any situation or location, *The Green Witch's Garden* allows you to experience the joy and reverence attached to overseeing life as it germinates, grows, and yields, and how to use the bounty in your magical practice.

How to Use This Book

FIRST OF ALL, this can't be a step-by-step guide. Growing zones, climates, and geological composition all vary widely across the world. In that sense, this book has to be a bit vague. I can suggest and offer you choices, but ultimately, your decisions will be grounded in the realities of your location. It will also depend on your personal vibe within your practice, meaning that if you're a potions person, telling you to grow tomatoes in your container garden because you can preserve them as sauce isn't going to help you much. This is a much more free-form book than the previous green witch books I've written. You'll find this one to be less prescriptive and more of a guideline for working intuitively within your own garden, according to your own choices.

Read it for ideas, to fill in your background, to help you have a better idea of where your materials come from. Remember: The most powerful magic you can create comes from you and your connection to your local energies. Work with your land, not against it.

While it can offer valuable spiritual insight and experience to nurture something from seed to healthy plant, this may not be possible for you. Taking an already established plant into your home can be just as beneficial to your practice. (Make sure to purify it; see Chapter 7 for ideas on how to accomplish this.) Not everyone has a green thumb. That's absolutely fine! You're not a failure as a green witch if you can't get seeds to start, or if you lose control over the process between germination and a seedling establishing itself securely. (If there's a stage that gives you a lot of trouble, however, meditate on it, and think about where it is in the life cycle of the plant. It may give you insight into your own spiritual insecurities or areas to strengthen in yourself.)

You don't have to have a greenhouse full of vibrant, fertile green things to qualify as a green witch. We all have different areas of strength. You can try growing all sorts of different plants, and you might discover that while you can't keep one kind alive, you do decently well with others. Find what you're best at and work from there.

Chapter 1

Green Witchcraft in the Garden

Why You Need a Garden for Your Craft

The natural world sings. Its rhythms thrum throughout our lives, entwined with our daily steps. It inspires, soothes, supports; it heals, whispers, and calms. It is understandable that we want to draw that rhythm into our homes or participate more personally in that song. It is one thing to walk through nature in a wild or public setting; it is another sort of experience to tend to nature one-on-one, to carefully and lovingly nurture and care for the green things that offer us life in return.

Gardening demonstrates to us that gentle care matters, even if only for a few moments every day or two. It is glaringly evident when we forget to tend our plants. Without our attention, they either droop or dry up or grow aggressively wild and threaten other plants. Regular care tailored to the plant's needs is important. It doesn't have to be complicated, but it does require a few moments from day to day, with occasional longer, more involved activity.

If that last sentence sounds like it could apply to your spiritual practice, then you're in good company. Touching base briefly with the Divine, reaching out to connect with the energy around you momentarily, is a form of self-care that can ground you. Every once in a while we take time to do more involved things like rituals or meditations to explore aspects of our personal growth. If we don't regularly engage in the brief moments of spiritual self-care, then the frequency of the larger, more involved activity has to increase to account for the lack of care in between, as there is more (and more difficult) work to be done.

If you ignore your plants for too long, you'll have a lot of work to do to bring them back to vibrant life. In this way, taking a daily moment to touch base with your plants serves as a spiritual check-in for you as well; interacting with your garden allows you to equalize your energy. It's a mutually beneficial relationship.

Interacting with green growing things is a learning experience. It's something that every green witch should try at least once, and preferably several times at various points in your life. Hands-on work with green living things is an incomparable way to connect with nature. Anyone can do it, and it can be done just about anywhere.

Working with a garden also offers you the chance to be mindful. The act of caring for your garden is an opportunity to be wholly in the moment, to disconnect from anxiety and stress to simply be and commune with another living thing. Handling and working with living things can also be a welcome change of focus from the negativity swirling around us in the world. Witches, empaths, and people who work with energy tend to be very affected by the state of the world, from being exposed to negativity, fear, and hopelessness both in the news and in their social surroundings. Gardening offers the chance to lower your blood pressure and increase serotonin levels.

Research has been done on a bacterium that lives in soil, *Mycobacterium vaccae,* that shows it stimulates the body to produce proteins that result in a decrease in stress and anxiety. The ingestion of this bacterium may have the same impact, so handling or consuming produce from your garden could also benefit you in this way.

If your garden is outside—whether you grow in containers, window boxes, or outdoor gardens—the act of being in fresh air also brings health benefits. Sunlight stimulates the production of vitamin D, which aids in the production of neurotransmitter regulators and thus helps stabilize moods; low levels of vitamin D may be associated with depression and anxiety. It also aids in calcium absorption and supports normal immune system function.

Managing your own garden also allows you the opportunity to influence and direct the energy development of specific plants. For example, lavender is often associated with purification, peace, harmony, and healing. As a gardener you may wish to encourage your lavender plant to lean specifically toward purification as it grows, in order to use it for that purpose later in your magical practice.

Other advantages of having your own garden include knowing that the plants you grow and use in your craft will be free of negative or unwanted energy, because they will have been grown in an environment controlled by you. You can also feel confident that plants grown under your surveillance will be free of chemicals and pesticides.

Your Garden As a Spiritual Reflection of You

Like spiritual work, gardening takes time and patience. Nothing is instantaneous. It is a very slow magic, one that you participate in as a gardener and witch. There are rarely earth-shattering revelations during gardening. Instead, there is a slow growth, learning that takes place over a longer stretch of time. Observing it can be an enlightening experience if you allow yourself to think of the garden as a metaphor for yourself.

There's a balance between controlling a garden and allowing it to go its own way, and it's one that every gardener has to find for themselves.

It depends on so many factors: what you choose to grow, the conditions, how you envision your garden, and so forth. Sometimes we expect order but can't keep up with the explosion of fertility and abundance. It's okay to revise your expectations and roll with what comes. The same applies to your spiritual journey: Sometimes unexpected things happen in your life that impact you and send you in a direction that you didn't foresee. Forcing yourself back to your original path can rob you of the growth that the new trajectory could have offered you. On the other hand, sometimes that new path might cost you too much, and returning to your original path is the healthier choice.

Houseplants and windowsill plants have cycles regardless of seasons. Watch them, make notes in your garden journal (see Chapter 5), and look for the patterns in your records over time.

The seasonal shift is slow, but you can really see it reflected in the changes of a garden. As the season unfolds, new tasks require your attention, and the opportunity to trace the shifts in energy throughout the continuous changes offers invaluable rewards. Likewise, you can better see shifts in your own energy as the season turns and you learn to predict how you respond to the larger cycle going on around you.

A garden also takes care and attention. You can't ignore it and expect everything to be orderly and perfect. The same goes for you. Self-care on physical, emotional, mental, and spiritual levels is essential, and it all starts with paying attention to yourself. Similarly, gardening requires different levels of care: Regular watering, weeding, and pruning are essential. Thinning out seedlings is important; if you don't cull some of the carrots that have sprouted, the others won't have room to grow. The green leafy tops will look lush, but under the ground, there will only be thin, spindly, pale roots.

On the other hand, leaving a garden to go wild yields a different kind of lesson. You'll get a result all right, and sometimes that result holds a message for you. There's a time for spontaneity, and a time for exercising judgment. Sometimes you have to let go of obsessively monitoring things every moment and just let nature go its way. Trust in the process. Listen to your intuition and listen to your garden.

Don't get bogged down in linking your garden too strongly to your own personality and how you see yourself. Also, don't see your garden's health or problems as directly indicative of your own, either current or forthcoming. Instead, see it as a spiritual parallel, a series of lessons to internalize and support your next effort.

Gardening work also helps clear the clutter and chatter of your mind. The manual labor helps unplug the mind from overthinking and encourages it to slow down and just be. Open yourself to insight and messages, and cultivate gratitude for the natural delights you encounter while you work. Your efforts in the garden help you focus on something outside yourself that parallels your own growing cycle and needs. You can also use your garden work as a meditative process. As you weed

The basics of grounding and centering can be found in *The Green Witch*. Essentially, the process has you locate your energy center within your body, then reach out from that energy center to connect with the energy of the earth. Through this connection you can equalize your energy level, borrowing some from the earth if you are low, or shunting excess energy to the earth if you are overloaded. You can also connect to the energy of the sky and equalize that way, although many find this a more difficult visualization and exchange of energy. Linking to both can offer a very secure connection.

the garden, for example, think about the little things in your life that draw energy away from your main focuses, the way weeds use space and nutrients you've earmarked for your plants. For more about meditation and your garden, see Chapter 9.

Building Your Connection to Nature

As green witches, we're constantly looking for ways to enhance our connection to nature. Gardening is one such way. Gardening, in whatever form, allows you to interact with the energy of nature through the observation of and participation with the life cycle of a plant. It offers more, however. It offers you a place to communicate with the elements, the four building blocks of nature, magic, and life itself, according to classical philosophers. Following is a basic exercise that allows you to isolate each element and respond to it within your garden space. Remember, this can be indoors or out, and it can be done any time you need to ground or otherwise calm yourself.

Recognizing the Natural Cycle

Birth, life, death. There is no beginning or ending to the natural life cycle. At any point, several cycles are occurring, each at different stages. Any point can be a beginning too. "It's the first day of the rest of your life" is a familiar phrase, and it's true. You can step aboard the cycle at any time and interact with it. Every moment is an experience.

Working with living plants is to interact with the natural birth-life-death-rebirth cycle. Nowhere is the cycle more apparent than after the growing season, when plants have died off and leaves and other remnants are raked and cleared out. This brings us to a very important part of the natural cycle of life that we don't discuss as often as we talk about growing things: decomposition, what occurs after death to all organic beings.

EXERCISE

The Elements and Your Garden

This is an exercise you can repeat frequently to help attune you to how the four elements function within your garden space. It's a good way to calm yourself if you're agitated or stressed, and a nice way to begin or end the day. If you're indoors, turn off your phone and any other distractions that may interrupt you. Take your time with each step; don't race through all four elements. Rushing defeats the purpose of the exercise. Sometimes you need time to sort through the energy in your space, which can shift from day to day depending on the weather, your mood, what kind of traffic or activity your garden has seen in the last few days, and so on.

1 First, settle yourself comfortably in your garden area. You can sit on the ground, use a chair, or sit any other way you feel comfortable. You may lie down if you like, but be aware that you may fall asleep!

2 Close your eyes and take three deep breaths, exhaling slowly after each.

3 Begin by reaching out to sense the element of earth. How does the surface beneath you feel? Can you isolate earth energy in the space around you? What does it feel like?

4 After a time, move to the element of air. What scents do you pick up from your garden space? Does the air move? How does it feel against your skin?

5 Move to sensing fire energy. Is there warmth in your space? What is the light like? Are there pockets or small areas of vitality or creative energy somewhere?

6 Finally, reach out to sense water energy. What is the level of humidity like in your garden space? Can you feel a difference in disparate zones?

7 When you feel ready, slowly draw back the personal energy you have used to sense the elemental energies at play in your garden space. Take a few deep, slow breaths and open your eyes when you feel ready. Take a moment to stretch and move your hands, feet, and limbs to seat yourself fully in your body again.

8 The last step is to make notes about your observations and experience in your grimoire, meditation record, spiritual journal, garden journal, or whatever you use to record your spiritual or magical work. Compare and contrast your comments with past notes on this exercise. Do you see patterns or rhythms?

Composting and decomposition is an important step in the natural cycle that allows you to interact with natural energy in a different way. We all know what it's like to be in nature and to feel surrounded by life. But the energy involved in the steps that occur after death is important, and just as worthy of interaction.

Gardening books talk about the function of compost, and how it can enrich your garden and growing matter. City collection of organic refuse for disposal and conversion to other uses is becoming more popular. But have you ever really considered the energy of compost? What does it create, what does it release?

Keeping a magical journal is very important. You can consult *The Green Witch's Grimoire* for an entire book exploring the ways you can organize and record information. See also the section in Chapter 5 on creating a garden journal, which can be part of your magical journal or a separate notebook, according to your preference.

Compost isn't garbage. It's a function of decomposition. Decomposition occurs after death, releasing energy as organic matter transforms to less structured matter, a form with nutrients more accessible to new organisms to use as building blocks in creating new life. The compost serves as nourishment and enrichment for future plants.

In nature, this happens without supervision. Walk through untended forested areas and see the leaves and fallen branches on the ground; look at the fallen logs that are crumbling and decomposing, hosts to fungi and mosses. Those plants plus bacteria, insects, and worms all work to break down the organic matter.

As green witches, we understand that decomposition is part of the natural cycle that should be worked with for insight. Many humans, on the other hand, tend to assume death is the end of the cycle, perhaps followed by rebirth in some form. This common belief overlooks and diminishes the importance of physical decomposition.

In some neo-pagan practices, Samhain, the third harvest, also marks the end of the cycle, a farewell, a release of what no longer serves us. The winter solstice marks the rebirth of the sun, and the cycle begins again.

But what happens in the weeks between Samhain and Yule? We think of fields lying fallow to recover energy, of incubating the seed that will manifest with the return of the sun. What is missing from this observance of the natural cycle? Decomposition.

It's not comfortable to think about or examine your life in the context of things breaking down and being reduced to base elements. But looking at the dark, uncomfortable parts of our spirituality and our practice of it is important. As witches, we know that dark things are not bad things. We know that darkness holds mystery and knowledge, secrets and revelations…if we are courageous enough to face them.

Decomposition releases energy, and transforms energy into simpler states, like untangling the building blocks that formed an energy structure. It unties and unravels, freeing the aggregate of energy to unwind and separate; the energy then becomes neutralized and ready to be reused.

This part of the cycle is introspective and meditative. It can be overwhelming, and there's nothing wrong with doing it a little bit at a time. You don't have to be shackled to the seasonal pattern, either, although working within the larger natural resonance of your geographical and agricultural location can make it easier. Composting happens all year long, with vegetable scraps in the winter, for example, or yard trimmings through the growing season.

Working with Plant Spirits

As witches, we honor the spirits of nature around us. Taking on care of a garden offers a new range of spirits to honor and work with. At the bare minimum, you should introduce yourself and welcome the spirit of the plant when you plant it or acquire it, or when it sprouts. (See Chapter 9 for more on working with plant spirits in your garden.)

As when you ask to work with a new animal spirit as a teacher, or choose to work with a specific deity to deepen your understanding of them and their spheres of influence, working with one plant spirit at a time is important. Don't overload yourself. Allow your focus to be given to one plant spirit at a time, in order to be as open as possible to their wisdom.

What are your favorite plants? Is there an herb or flower that resonates strongly with you? Try one of those as the first plant spirit you work with. This basic technique for communicating with a plant spirit will help you get started.

1. Center and ground, in order to have a firm foundation for your own energy.
2. Spend a bit of time looking at the plant, familiarizing yourself with the details of its physical structure.
3. Reach out with your personal energy and touch the energy of the plant. What does it feel like? Ask yourself if it feels welcoming or not. If it doesn't, terminate the exercise and try again another time. If it feels neutral or agreeable, proceed.
4. Close your eyes and visualize the plant before you. Introduce yourself (aloud or in your visualization) and ask the spirit if it is willing to meet you and communicate. Again, if you get a sense of refusal or reluctance, thank it and withdraw. If the spirit is amenable, proceed.
5. Ask the spirit if it is willing to teach you. Be open to whatever messages it wishes to communicate. Remember to thank the spirit at the end of each session.

This sharing may take place over an extended period of time. Care for the plant as you learn from it, make it offerings of whatever it seems to like (water? shiny crystals? rocks? music?), and acknowledge your gratitude frequently. Also be aware that the plant may just want to hang out. It might not have something to communicate, but it may enjoy your company. As you get to know its energy, you may want to just hang out with it too.

As part of your deep dive into a plant's energies, whether you are communicating with the plant spirit or not, care for it with awareness. Don't just water it and turn its pot; allow your energy to reach out and touch the plant's energy every time you care for it. The spoken word creates sound waves, which plants can physically feel, much the way your eardrum vibrates when sound waves hit it. We project energy when we speak too; emotion and other kinds of energy infuse our words. Plants, being organic creatures with energy of their own, can respond to that.

> Make it personal. Talking to plants is a cliché, but there's truth behind it.

Eco-Awareness

As green witches, we are caretakers and guardians of the land. We help nature's energy move and facilitate people's interactions with it. Understanding that we are inextricably entwined with the world of plants is essential to our work. Eliot Cowan, author of *Plant Spirit Medicine*, makes this observation about the relationship between humans and plants:

> The most striking thing about this relationship is that we need them but they don't need us. We humans are utterly dependent on plants to cover all our needs: fuel, shelter, clothing, medicine, the petrochemical cornucopia, and, of course, food. (Even meat is made of plants.) In contrast, plant communities do just fine without people.…What makes plants so generous? What makes us so brutal? Somewhere along the way we lost the experience of unity.

Nature does quite well without us, true. But the interference and stress humans put on the planet in general calls for us to contribute support to the natural world whenever we can.

How can you do this in your garden? Practice eco-awareness as much as possible. An awareness of environmental issues, both global and local, should inform your choices. This applies to choices made beyond your garden; it should influence the food you buy, the companies you support, and the activist groups you assist in whatever way(s) you can. For example:

- Does a vegetable gardener use harsh techniques that strip the soil and fail to nourish it in return, resulting in increasingly artificial methods to amplify harvest?
- Where are the ingredients in your favorite spreads sourced?
- Is an ingredient produced in a way that diminishes the environment it comes from? Is the cocoa you use in baking fair trade?

You can also support pollinators. This means having native wildflowers, perennials that are there for these beneficial creatures year after year, including milkweed, thistle, asters, and many others (remember to choose plants that grow in your unique environment). Try to plant things that attract specific pollinators too, like milkweed for monarch butterflies or wildflowers to support local honeybee populations. Which specific pollinators to support will depend on your geographic location, but in general, butterflies, bees, and insects function as pollinators, among other animals. A decrease in pollinator population can have significant consequences for the global food supply. Pollinator populations suffer when the native plants they prefer die or are no longer planted; their numbers also decline as a result of contact with pests, pesticides, and toxic agrochemicals. Habitat loss is another factor that challenges pollinator survival, and you can help to restore that habitat with your garden.

In addition to providing support for pollinator species, you can practice eco-awareness by being a good steward of the soil. Plant a diverse range of things to provide a good cross-section of plants that consume different minerals and nutrients from the soil, as well as provide a variety to return to it after composting. In this way, your use of soil is more efficient, as is the creation of the compost that will in turn feed it again. Adding a variety of organic material to the compost will also enrich it further; kitchen waste such as vegetable and fruit waste, coffee grounds and tea leaves, and eggshells can all add valuable nutrients that will support future growth when the compost is mixed with garden soil the next season.

Dispose of leaf litter, grass clippings, and garden cuttings on your property instead of bagging them for collection. These things offer food and shelter for insects and birds. (If you use real Christmas or Yule trees and/or boughs as decoration around the winter solstice, leave these outside; they make excellent shelter during the snowy season.) You can compost these things, or leave them to decompose in place in the garden. Leaving leaf litter on the ground instead of raking it up is becoming a more widespread practice, as it provides organic matter for decomposition that enriches the soil, as well as shelter for small creatures.

Regenerative Gardening

Regenerative gardening is a practice that replaces the nutrients in the soil that are used up by growing plants. This is done to improve the next round of plants to grow in that place, as well as to increase the nutrients that will be consumed by us if these plants are edible. It's a practice that has positive benefits for the environment. It stimulates plant growth and enhances biodiversity. You can practice regenerative gardening to various degrees in your garden space, depending on your environment and your needs.

Part of regenerative gardening involves planting supportive plants to foster pollinators and beneficial insects nearby.

This type of holistic agricultural technique seeks to reverse the nutrient stripping that commercial agricultural practices have caused. It also better supports the water cycle and improves carbon drawdown (plants are a natural way to pull carbon from the air via photosynthesis). Regenerative gardening simply means returning organic matter to the tired soil, which is, in essence, what we do when we add composted material to our gardening soil. In addition, regenerative gardening doesn't use tilling, the technique of stirring up the soil to loosen it in preparation for planting or to break up weeds that are sprouting. Tilling exposes more soil to the air, where it releases carbon. Loss of carbon in soil weakens its structure, fertility, and ability to hold water, all things growing plants require.

Regenerative gardening also looks to reduce exhausted soil through crop rotation, or sowing different plants annually in a specific place. Different plants use different nutrients and minerals in the soil, so planting the same kind of crop in the same location every year strips the soil of a specific set of nutrients more quickly.

It may sound like this is the kind of thing large-scale crop producers can focus on, but as witches we can take these ideas and work with them on a smaller scale. Here are some ideas that may help you to be a more regenerative gardener:

- **Use cover crops.** The idea behind cover crops is growing plants specifically to plow them into the soil, adding fresh greens to the earth where they will decompose and add a rich variety of nutrients. This differs from using compost in that compost is already broken down (or mostly so) when it is mixed into the soil; energy has already been released. With fresh greens, the entire decomposition cycle happens in the soil itself.
- **Limit soil exposure.** If you harvest a plant and pull up the remaining plant matter, have something else ready to plant in its place. This keeps the time soil is exposed to a minimum. Likewise, you can cover areas with nothing planted in them with straw, mulch, or landscape fabric to help protect the soil.

- ❧ **Practice zero tilling.** Tilling breaks up the integrity of the soil, thereby disturbing its ability to hold water and resist erosion. It also exposes the soil, which then releases carbon into the air. As an alternative to tilling, cover the soil around your plants with straw, mulch, or landscape fabric, and loosen earth by inserting a garden fork into the ground over and over, without lifting the soil and turning it over to expose the underside.

- ❧ **Fertilize responsibly.** Fertilizer refreshes soil and adds back the nutrients it has lost to previous plants growing in it. Instead of purchasing chemical-based fertilizer from the garden center, use your compost. Various food wastes can add the nutrients needed by particular plants, and you can mix nutritious fertilizing teas from things in your pantry. Eggshells, coffee grounds, and fireplace ash are all common elements of homemade fertilizer mixes. There are some easy DIY fertilizer recipes available at "15 Organic DIY Garden Fertilizer Recipes That'll Beautify Your Garden" on DIYnCrafts .com (www.diyncrafts.com/22484/home/ gardening/15-organic-diy-garden-fertilizer- recipes-thatll-beautify-garden).

There are organic-based fertilizers available for purchase, but you may have ethical problems with them. Common fertilizers include blood meal and bone meal, both excellent for soil, but that are generally sourced from slaughterhouses. Manure is another common and easily obtained fertilizer, but if you're vegan, using animal refuse may make you uncomfortable, as it may be tainted with blood, feathers, or other animal products.

Regenerative gardening acknowledges the interconnectedness of nature, the web of energies that encompasses the world and those who live in it. Nothing you do in a garden is done in a vacuum. Garden with awareness and make the best choices you can for your plants and your land.

Alternative Gardens

Perhaps you don't have the funds or energy to have your own garden. You may not live in a space that allows you to have houseplants or a container garden. If you rent a room, you can be limited as to what you do, depending on house rules or how permanent your situation is. With that in mind, here are some alternative things you could do to create a garden.

GROW CUTTINGS FROM VEGETABLE SCRAPS

Growing from vegetable scraps reduces food waste, can save money, and allows you the experience of both growing things and eating them. It's also a form of reclaiming. These scraps would normally be thrown away. By making something new out of them, you're transforming; it's a very green witch thing to do. See Chapter 4 for information on how to grow plants from vegetable cuttings.

COMMUNITY GARDENS

Some cities and towns have public areas you can sign up for to plant a garden for non-commercial use. Generally, these are for growing food, but some may also be for beautification, and you may be able to mix the two.

Community gardens may have rules to be followed regarding your participation. For example, you might have to donate something, or log a certain number of hours working on common areas at the garden. The garden may be overseen by a volunteer committee.

Check your city's website for information about community garden plots. You may have to put your name on a waiting list, as these are often in demand. If you live in a residence of some kind, there may be a communal outdoor space managed by the residents. (If there isn't, ask the owners/management if you can organize one!) Generally, a community garden area will have some sort of annual fee associated with it to cover the costs of materials and overall upkeep.

The benefits of working with a community garden can include advice from gardening instructors who tour the city's gardens, learning from other gardeners, sharing costs, and an increased connection among neighborhood residents. Community gardens also increase the green space of the area, reclaiming land that might otherwise be vacant. On top of all this, community gardens encourage people to get outdoors, and support mental and physical well-being.

GUERRILLA GARDENING

Guerrilla gardening is gardening on land you don't own and/or don't have permission to use. Empty overgrown lots, public land that isn't being cultivated, or any municipal area that isn't specifically set aside for gardening use can be a location for guerrilla gardening. Guerrilla gardening can be as easy as planting flowers around a civic tree, or as complex as planting a full vegetable garden along a railway track or the legally mandated clearance space surrounding high-voltage power lines.

Guerrilla gardening has a certain special feeling to it. At any moment, the garden could vanish. It's ephemeral, liminal. It's quite magical in that you are making something from nothing, using space that would otherwise be blank to create food or beauty. At the same time, there is the risk that you could lose hours or even years of work. If you think of the gain in the meantime, however, it can be very satisfying to engage in working with the land.

If you are drawn to the idea of beautifying a vacant space but don't have the ability to garden it due to financial or physical limitations, the "seed bomb" is a beloved tool of guerrilla gardeners that is inexpensive and easy to create and use. A seed bomb is a small ball of seeds, compost, and clay that you toss into a space and allow to germinate and grow. It's a more successful way of scattering seed over an area; it protects the seeds from being blown away or eaten by birds, and allows them to germinate safely. Several small balls are more successful than a few larger ones. Search online for seed bomb recipes and remember to use plants native to your area; introducing invasive species is dangerous, and using plants that can't grow in your climate is pointless.

COMMUNITY-SUPPORTED AGRICULTURE

If you are interested in fresh food but can't grow it due to physical or other limitations, look into supporting a local program that works with farmers and cultivators in your area.

Community-supported agriculture (CSA) is a form of subscription to a specific farm or groups of farmers in which you pay a certain amount and receive shares of the farm's produce on a regular basis in return. This allows you to directly support the local agricultural economy and use seasonal produce as it is harvested, another way to be in touch with your local seasonal growing cycle. The farms often keep in touch with their subscribers via newsletters and in person at the weekly pickup, and some offer community days where subscribers can participate in harvesting or maintenance, or allow regular labor in exchange for part of the subscription cost. This kind of farm share can also be found for meat-producing farms, baked goods, eggs and dairy, and more.

Chapter 2

Magical Goals for Your Garden

How Will You Use Your Garden?

Before you begin planning your garden, think about what you want your end result to be. Like spellcraft, it's important to clearly define your goal before you start so you can fine-tune each step to support that aim.

As you read through this chapter, you may not have a very clear concept of what you want your garden to be. You might want a bit of everything. There's nothing wrong with that. If your goal is to just grow stuff in order to be hands-on and participate in the energy cycles associated with nature, then that's fine! My family's garden is very much a mishmash of a few vegetables and lots of flowers, shrubs, and herbs. It doesn't have a cohesive theme other than being a place we enjoy. It *does* have specific magical benefits that we recognize, though, and I'll cover some of them here.

In designing your garden, especially if your space is limited, you have to make decisions regarding what role (or roles) you want your garden to serve in your spiritual and magical work. You can't have everything…but there are ways in which plants can serve double duty or even multiple roles.

Don't panic. This isn't a one-time kind of decision! The wonderful thing about plants is that they have a natural life cycle. Annuals last a single season. Perennials return again and again, growing back after dying off at the end of their growing season or going dormant. By its very nature, a garden is an ever-changing, evolving thing. Your garden isn't carved in stone, nor should it be.

Something not being addressed here is how to garden within a certain budget. It's very easy to wander through a greenhouse nursery and be overwhelmed by the choices and the cost of supplies and tools. Naturally your choices and decisions will be affected by the budget you set for yourself. However, it's important to remember that you can create a garden from discards and vegetable scraps, by making rootings from cuttings of herbs, or by taking cuttings from other plants, either wild or owned by acquaintances. It isn't necessary to spend hundreds of dollars and devote a lot of land to your garden project.

If you already have a garden, then take stock of it. What do you have that you want to keep? What do you want to remove in order to have space and resources for something else that you have more use for? If you want to keep something, but not where it currently is, then mark it to be moved. See later in this chapter for more on working with an existing garden.

PLANNING STAGE: MAGICAL

The magical aspect of planning your garden is almost exactly like planning out a spell.

1. **First, define your intentions.** What is your goal for this garden? Are you going to grow food? Are you going to grow spell ingredients? Is it going to be a place for relaxation?

2. **Next, outline your goals.** Your goals might include introducing new plants you've never worked with before, starting certain plants from seed, transforming the energy of your growing space into something more supportive and healthy, or increasing your ability to communicate with plants. If you like, you can make a list of short-term goals and long-term goals.

3. **Then write out your vision in detail.** As when you plan a spell, you want to be as clear and detailed as possible. Going into any magical endeavor with only a vague idea of what you want will make it difficult for you to follow through. Conversely, if you really like spontaneity, you can intentionally go into your magical planning with undefined goals; you'll have to roll with whatever happens, which can be a great learning experience, but it can also be costly in terms of time and money. A detailed vision helps you keep focus and allows you to direct your magical energy efficiently.

PLANNING STAGE: PRACTICAL

This stage is where you do the real-life planning to help bring about your magical goals. Before planting a garden, you need to know:

- What the growing zone is for your geographic location
- What your soil composition is like
- What kind of weather your area has
- What kind of plants you'd like to grow (your choices here will be determined by the data you gather regarding all the other points)

Let's look at why this information is important.

ZONES

Hardiness zones or growing zones can help you eliminate a lot of plants right off the bat, simply because they won't thrive in your location. It's why you don't see palm trees in the Arctic. Plants develop in specific climates in response to what that climate offers and provides. A simple growing zone map will help you identify the average low temperatures in your area so you can get plants that are suited for that climate. This map doesn't include information on rainfall and other measures, but it's still a vital tool in your planning.

Growing zones are excellent guides for green witches. They highlight what resonates with the energy of your geographic position. They'll stop you from trying to force something unsuitable for your climate to grow there, which uses up a lot of energy that could probably be better directed elsewhere. Witches work with the energies of their environments, not against them.

There are ways around growing zone restrictions. Gardening indoors or having a greenhouse can help extend your growing zone, opening up the possibility of a more varied selection of plants. However, unless you invest a lot of money in it, you won't be able to perfectly reproduce the conditions required by plants zoned for a very different climate. (See Hardiness Zones at the end of this book for more information.)

SOIL

The composition of the soil in your chosen garden area is also critical. The chemical composition of soil—including whether it's sandy or full of organic material, the topography of the land, and the sufficient presence of living organisms dictate the quality of soil, thereby influencing what plants will be able to survive in it. Soil has to have the right amount of air, water, and organic and inorganic materials to sustain life.

Sometimes the soil quality and/or composition can be improved by introducing topsoil. Topsoil is a nutrient-rich layer of soil that makes up approximately the top eight inches of earth, resting atop the deeper layer known as subsoil. Topsoil has a high concentration of the microorganisms and humus required for plant growth. It can be purchased from garden centers in bags or delivered in bulk.

The average soil is composed of several different elements. It's roughly 45 percent inorganic matter, 25 percent air, 25 percent water, and about 5 percent organic matter. The organic matter (also called humus) is made up of microorganisms and decayed or decaying plant and animal matter. Inorganic matter is made of various sizes of rock particles.

Topsoil can lose its nutritive value and depreciate over time as the nutrients are consumed by plant growth, affected by erosion, and filtered by rainfall and other water. Adding a bit of new topsoil every couple of years can help rejuvenate the existing garden area—as can adding compost, which reintroduces the nutrients that decaying plant matter provides.

There's other important information to gather about your soil, such as its condition. Does your soil have a high amount of clay? Is it very dry or extremely wet? Is it acidic or alkaline? Talk to your local gardening center to find out more about the natural soil in your area. You can also call your local county extension office; some extension offices provide soil testing services.

WEATHER

Any gardener will tell you: The weather is important. Growing zones are focused on temperatures, but there are many other factors that will affect your success. Look at the weather patterns of your location to get more insight into what your plants will be facing. Is your area very humid? Are you near water, which will affect how storms roll through and what kind of precipitation they can drop? Things like large hills, valleys, and other geological features can impact the weather that hits an area, redirecting wind and storm movement. The weather that hits you can be very different from the weather that a town ten minutes to the north or south experiences.

Modifying an Existing Garden

If you already have some kind of garden and want to adapt it to be more magical, then you'll need to take stock of what's already there. Ask yourself the following questions:

- ❧ What plants do I have that serve a magical purpose? Look up correspondences for them and explore their energies to gain a sense of what they mean to you personally.
- ❧ What existing plants can I move or remove to give myself space for plants I choose specifically for magical purposes?
- ❧ What plants can I add to complement the ones I already have?

Another idea is to rededicate your existing space to be specifically a magical garden. In all likelihood, this would be a confirmation of how you've already been using it. Green witches use what's at hand, and everything is considered magical, after all. We don't require specialized spaces in order to follow our paths. However, dedicating your space to being a magical garden can help the energies coalesce and be more actively supportive of your magical goals. A dedication links the space to you in a more structured way.

It's possible that you've already developed a relationship with your garden space, and that's terrific. A dedication can be like an official recognition of the existing relationship.

Rededicating the space can be especially useful if you're setting out to redesign your garden with magical and/or spiritual work in mind. Think of it as a magical reorientation. To do this, you need to evaluate the existing energy of the space as a whole. This is a different process than looking at the individual plants, as you did earlier in this chapter. This evaluation takes in the energy of the space itself. As you know, this energy will be a combination of many things, including those plants that currently occupy it. Ask yourself what you like about it, and what you would like to change. Write your garden rededication focusing on enhancing the energies you want to keep and inviting the energies you wish to replace those that are undesired.

What about the existing energy that you don't want to keep? Thank it for its work in the past and wish it well as it finds somewhere new. Energy can be transformed, so another way to deal with this is to reprogram the energy of the space in a way of your choosing: Use stones or crystals to help influence the energy, burn dried herbs carrying the desired energy, make and bury charms to attract the preferred energy, and so forth.

A Garden for Cooking and Food

Are you a kitchen-focused witch? Is food one of your love languages? You may be looking to support that aspect of your craft by producing ingredients and seasonings. A garden like this will focus on vegetables and herbs, possibly with some fruit-bearing trees or shrubs if you have the space and are in a favorable hardiness zone.

What should you plant? Keep these things in mind:

- What do you cook most? There's no point in planting a slew of vegetables if you don't cook meals that involve those specific kinds of plants.
- What preserves well? Think about your storage space. It's useless to grow a zillion tomatoes if you don't have the equipment to process them or the space to store the jars you put them in.

🌿 What do you have room for? Think about your garden space too. If you're short of planting area, focus more on the seasonings you use. There's nothing wrong with buying your produce from the farmer's market and using your garden onions, garlic, and herbs when you cook with them.

Some food-bearing plants, such as strawberries, tomatoes, potatoes, and herbs, do well in container gardens. Containers can add to your growing space or be the entire growing space if your garden area is limited to a balcony or porch. See Chapter 4 for ideas about indoor gardens too.

A basic selection of herbs in a magical garden designed to be a source for magical cooking might include:

🌿 Basil
🌿 Coriander/cilantro
🌿 Dill
🌿 Mint
🌿 Oregano

🌿 Parsley
🌿 Rosemary
🌿 Sage
🌿 Tarragon
🌿 Thyme

Basic vegetables in a green witch's garden might include:

🌿 Beans
🌿 Broccoli
🌿 Brussels sprouts
🌿 Cabbage
🌿 Carrots
🌿 Celery
🌿 Corn
🌿 Cucumbers
🌿 Greens such as kale, chard, various lettuces

🌿 Onions
🌿 Parsnips
🌿 Peas
🌿 Peppers
🌿 Potatoes
🌿 Radishes
🌿 Squash
🌿 Tomatoes
🌿 Zucchini

EDIBLE FLOWERS

Who says a food garden can't have flowers as well? As well as not needing a reason to add beauty to your garden, certain flowers are edible, as long as they haven't been treated with chemicals at some point. Other flowers, like marigolds (which are also edible themselves), can be planted alongside food-bearing plants to help deter insects. Here is a selection of edible flowers:

- Borage
- Clover
- Honeysuckle
- Impatiens
- Nasturtiums
- Roses
- Violets

A Garden to Grow Magical Elements

If your witchcraft focuses on spellwork and you use plant matter in your magical work, consider developing a garden to source spell supplies. To do this, ask yourself some questions to help determine what to plant.

Bonus points if you find a plant suitable for your hardiness zone and physical situation that covers more than one magical goal. Most plants have multiple correspondences to begin with, so choosing a versatile plant that plays multiple roles isn't just convenient—it's downright clever.

1. Look at your most-reached-for supplies. What do you use most frequently? What do you need to replace regularly? Once you have this list, do a bit of research to find out if those plants grow in your hardiness zone. (For more on hardiness zones, see earlier in this chapter, as well as Hardiness Zones later in this book.) If the plants in question do grow in your hardiness zone, do they require specific conditions that your soil/position/weather cannot supply? If they do require conditions you cannot provide, are there plants that can serve as analogues or replacements for these plants' magical energies?

2. Look at the type of magical goals you work for most frequently. Choose zone-friendly plants that support these goals.

3. Design a garden with a selection of appropriate plants that cover a range of magical goals. This allows you to have a choice among several when a need arises.

A Magical Oasis Garden

A magical oasis garden offers you the opportunity to design and enjoy a place that answers your needs. Whatever you envision as an oasis—something rejuvenating, something restful, something cheerful or sedate—you can design it and create it. And then, of course, you get to take pleasure in it.

This type of garden, perhaps more than any other, is a reflection of you and your needs. Caring for it can become an analogy for caring for yourself. As cautioned in Chapter 1, though, don't let this analogy go too far. If the garden doesn't prosper, don't map that onto what might happen to you, or interpret it to mean you are a failure as well. Instead, look at what message the garden may be sending you. Did it need more water or less? Did you choose the right kind of plants for your zone and the physical kind of garden you're making (container, indoor, and so forth)? Did you pay attention to the weather and adjust your care accordingly? Designating your garden as a magical oasis, created just the way you dream of it, is a way of caring for yourself and caring for the earth as well.

Do you want your garden to be built around one theme, or do you want different magical zones to all add up to an overall oasis? There are no rules. Choose what makes you happy!

To help you pin down what your oasis garden would look like, think about the kind of environment you find refreshing, soothing, safe, or whatever feeling you're looking for. Whether it's peace, joy, healing, or security you desire, you can create an oasis garden that will fulfill your wishes.

This kind of garden is so personal a reflection of you and your needs that there isn't much more guidance I can provide here. A magical oasis garden can't be prescribed for you. I invite you to meditate and open yourself to inspiration and guidance from the universe as you work through designing it. The rest of this book can support you in your process, offering ideas, concepts, and information. Trust your intuition.

An Oasis for Native Species

As a green witch, you know that working with location-specific native plants carries significant resonance. Geography determines what plants you can and cannot grow in your garden. Stewardship of the earth involves acting on behalf of the planet and species that are struggling as a result of humankind's interference. Why not design your magical oasis to support them?

Choose native or heirloom plants that serve as food and shelter for birds, butterflies, beneficial insects, and bees. In general, pollinators are drawn to brightly colored flowers (lots of them!) and fragrant blooms. Planting a variety of plants that flower at different times provides an ongoing supply of nectar and pollen for the species that need them.

Pollinators, especially bees, like flowers such as the following, which are easy to grow in most hardiness zones. Bonus: These plants have medicinal benefits and magical benefits too:

- Borage
- Catnip
- Coneflower
- Cornflower
- Fennel
- Heather
- Hyssop
- Lavender
- Primrose
- Sunflower
- Yarrow

Rewilding

When planning out your garden area you might want to consider rewilding. Rewilding is the process of turning lawns into more vibrant, healthy, and environmentally supportive garden areas. A lawn has no reason to exist these days other than to be decorative; it is a concept left over from a time when an area covered with cultivated grass signified that you were wealthy enough to have land to spare (meaning you didn't need to use it to grow food or crops for money).

Unfortunately, emerald lawns, while looking clean and neat, do nothing for the health of the soil, nor do they provide a habitat or resources for pollinators. One of today's very real crises is a water shortage, which threatens wild lands and human-inhabited areas alike. Keeping a lawn green requires large amounts of water, a resource that is wasted for no reason other than to make a purely decorative statement...and a ground cover that has absolutely zero benefit beyond that.

Bonus: You don't have to mow your lawn if you remove the grass entirely and use the space for alternative ground covers. Take a look at Chapter 6 for some ideas for non-lawn ground cover.

Rewilding turns these dead-end lawns into thriving habitats for the pollinator population, as well as beautifying it. First steps can be as easy as ceasing the use of chemical-based growth aids or pest control. Raise the blades on the lawn mower to leave existing grass more room to grow, thereby shading the earth beneath and providing shelter for insects. Start sprinkling clover seed or another appropriate native ground cover over the ground in spring instead of grass seed. Don't weed the lawn unless what pops up is an invasive non-native plant. (Benign neglect is a valid technique here!) Take more space from the lawn area and give it to garden space for native species that support pollinators and other native species.

Chapter 3

Kinds of Witch Gardens

Basic Components of a Green Witch Garden

At its heart, your green witch garden should provide you with two things:

1. The opportunity to be hands-on with the natural cycle
2. The energy to contribute to filling your daily needs and your magic

Let's look at both of these components in more depth.

HANDS-ON WITH THE NATURAL CYCLE

Observing something allows you to gain insight into it. Learning to pay attention to small shifts or changes and respond to them is a valuable skill for a witch to develop. We tend to think of change in sweeping visions. However, the world doesn't work like that. Changes tend to be very small—shifts that are barely noticeable on their own. It's only when a series of small shifts causes enough deviation from the previous state that we generally notice.

The more you practice observing something day to day (or even hour by hour), the better you will get at recognizing minute changes. This in turn increases your sensitivity to subtle energy work.

Time spent working on your observation skills is never wasted.

Apart from allowing you to participate physically in the growing cycle by engaging in the process of caring for plants, observing the natural cycle in a garden allows you insight into the shifting energies of that cycle. It offers you the chance to reflect on the slow movement of energy and how it affects you, your own energies, and the changes in your own life.

ACCESS TO ENERGY

All living things produce and consume energy. As witches, we use the energy of color, stones, sigils, and plants (among other things) to help us influence our energy and the energy of our surroundings to achieve certain goals.

Having access to a garden, no matter what the size, indoors or outdoors, means that you have access to an ongoing energy source. To a witch, this is invaluable. You know about enhancing and affecting the energy of a space by adding rocks or plants or colors to shape or influence it more toward your vision or need. With a garden, you can use the energy produced by the living plants in much the same way you can borrow energy from the earth.

You don't necessarily have to harvest plant matter to use its energy. Surprised? People tend to think of a spell component as something that gets used up, especially organic materials like flowers or leaves or seeds. I suspect this comes from the fact that organic matter eventually decomposes anyway. Perhaps it's because spells often ask for a measured amount of plant matter, like recipes do, or because the plant matter is often burned or sewn into a charm bag. It can be seen as an offering or sacrifice. However, the energy of plants can be drawn on while they live, as well. You can either draw on a specific plant's energy (such as protection or love) or use the generic living energy to add to your magical working. See Chapter 9 for an exploration of this concept.

Astrological Gardens

Astrology is a system that interests some witches deeply, and planetary energy has been applied to herbalism and plant classification for centuries. There are several different ways in which astrology can be involved in gardening. First, let's look at planting by astrological associations.

If you look at collections of older herbal knowledge—Culpeper, for instance—you'll see that each plant was associated with a celestial body. This was generally done by examining the plant and assigning it a planetary classification based on the physical look of the plant, its scent, life cycle, what sort of medical issues it treated, and other factors.

There are seven classical planets because that's all that the ancients were aware of at the time. Modern planets such as Neptune and Uranus weren't revealed until our technology could perceive them. The seven classical planets also are not all planets—two are our luminaries, the sun and the moon. The seven classical celestial bodies, their attributes and energies, and their plant associations are:

- **Saturn:** boundaries, binding, banishing, elders, aging, death; plants that are poisonous, shade-loving, or grow in poor ground; plants with bad scents; plants that affect the excretory system, bones
- **Jupiter:** generosity, law; plants that affect the digestive system, liver, blood vessels; plants that are large; plants that are nutritious, appetizing
- **Mars:** defense, attack, vitality; plants with thorns or prickly stems or leaves, spicy scents; plants that affect the immune system, blood, sex drive
- **Venus:** love, prosperity, aphrodisiacs; plants that affect the urinary system, plants that affect genitals, plants that heal wounds; plants with velvety leaves, sweet scents
- **Mercury:** knowledge, travel, communication, divination; plants with feathery leaves, short intense scents; plants that affect the respiratory and nervous systems
- **Sun:** wealth, protection, health; plants affecting the circulatory system, eyesight, antidepressants; plants with yellow or orange flowers, citrusy scents
- **Moon:** clairvoyance, psychic ability; sedative plants; plants that open at or after sundown, plants with high water content

One of the easiest ways to plan out an astrological garden is to plant seven zones in your garden space and select plants associated with each planet/luminary to plant in each. The outcome of this is a good cross-section of plants. Planted together in groups, they can strengthen the astrological energy associated with the planet/luminary they're classified under.

Using Astrology to Time Gardening

Choosing when to undertake an action depending on the best suited astrological time for that action is called electional astrology. There are two common ways to time your gardening actions astrologically: according to planetary hours and by the lunar transit.

Astrological Garden

Planetary Hours

Planetary hours are a very precise way of scheduling an activity or event to take advantage of the most favorable astrological time. This symbolic system assigns a planet to a period of time (called an hour but doesn't correspond to the mundane sixty-minute hour), positing that this hour carries energy that resonates with the ruling celestial body associated with it.

Seven celestial bodies rule the hours of the day. The order is the same, but which planet begins the sequence depends on the day of the week. Each day will begin with the planet the day of the week is named for:

- Sunday: sun
- Monday: moon
- Tuesday: Mars
- Wednesday: Mercury
- Thursday: Jupiter
- Friday: Venus
- Saturday: Saturn

The length of a planetary hour is different every day; each "hour" constitutes a calculated portion of daylight time. The system posits twelve hours in a day and twelve in a night. However, because the duration of daytime and nighttime shift fluidly from day to day, how long a diurnal planetary hour lasts will reflect one-twelfth of those daylight hours.

The order of the planets for planetary hours doesn't follow the days of the week, however. It's organized by how close the classical planets in the sky appeared to Earth, ordered from farthest to closest: Saturn, Jupiter, Mars, the sun, Venus, Mercury, and the moon.

To calculate your planetary hours, all you need to know is the time of sunrise and sunset for your location. Calculate the total amount of time between sunrise and sunset, then divide that number by twelve. This will be the length of a diurnal planetary hour. Repeat the process for the nocturnal hours using the time of sunset and the time of sunrise the following morning.

The seven hours are associated with different energies. You'll recognize the general sense of them, as you've seen similar lists earlier in this chapter.

- **Hour of Saturn:** Organizing, sticking to tedious work that needs to get done, rest and introspection, breaking bad habits. Garden maintenance like weeding or whatever part of garden work you enjoy the least could be done in the hour of Saturn.

- **Hour of Jupiter:** Success, launching new projects. Anything that you're trying for the first time and want every chance of it succeeding is good to do in the hour of Jupiter. Likewise, setting out seedlings or starting seeds would also be good activities.

- **Hour of Mars:** Physical activities, things that require courage, grounded confrontation (as long as your emotions aren't running high; Mars can very easily go overboard). Is there a particularly pesky rabbit, deer, or groundhog interfering with your garden? Setting out measures to deal with them would be appropriate for a Mars hour. Building new fences or repairing beds would also be good choices.

- **Hour of the Sun:** Success, particularly in career-associated domains, employment in general, improving health. Working with plants associated with healing and/or success is a good choice for a Sun hour.

- **Hour of Venus:** Relationships, love, marriage, financial investment, reconciliation, serenity. Working to beautify the garden and making gardening decisions associated with your budget are appropriate during an hour of Venus.

- **Hour of Mercury:** Mental activity, communication, signing contracts, technology. Mercury hours are good for planning and evaluating how your garden is doing, and making decisions regarding your next steps or future plans.

- **Hour of the Moon:** Intuition, creativity, domestic activity. General garden maintenance is always appropriate during an hour of the Moon. Designing and tweaking your garden according to your heart and preferences are also Moon hour types of work.

THE LUNAR TRANSIT

Established by Babylonian astronomers around 400 B.C.E., the zodiac is an area of the sky through which the sun appears to travel throughout the year. It's divided into zones that are named for the major constellations that appear in the zones.

Unlike planetary hours, the time the moon spends in relation to each planet is approximately forty-eight hours. The moon connects with all twelve planets associated with the zodiac in its twenty-eight-day cycle. The "void of course" moon occurs after the moon makes its final major aspect with another planet before changing signs.

The energies of each planet influence the moon's energy, acting like a filter or a colored shade placed over a lamp. The lamp is still there, but the light it casts will be tinted the color of the shade.

Here are the twelve astrological signs and their ruling planets. (The more recently discovered planets are listed first, and the previous classical association is in parentheses.)

- Aries: Mars
- Taurus: Venus
- Gemini: Mercury
- Cancer: Moon
- Leo: Sun
- Virgo: Mercury
- Libra: Venus
- Scorpio: Pluto (Mars)
- Sagittarius: Jupiter
- Capricorn: Saturn
- Aquarius: Uranus (Saturn)
- Pisces: Neptune (Jupiter)

When the moon is void of course, it isn't close to—therefore is not being influenced by—any of the planets associated with the astrological house along the zodiac path. It's not in either the previous sign or the upcoming sign, and therefore is not being influenced by either of the associated planets. It's an introspective time for the moon. It generally doesn't last for very long—often only minutes or a couple of hours—but every once in a while, because of how the planets are positioned in the sky, the moon can be void of course for a day or so.

A void of course moon can leave us feeling ungrounded or out of focus. It can be compared to a planet in retrograde in that it can muddy things up for a bit. It's a good time for self-care and taking a step away from the rush of life. What does this mean for your garden? It means you can select the best time for performing certain actions, such as planting, pruning, fertilizing, or harvesting. You can take the best moon phase (see the next section) and, within that moon phase, look at the different houses the moon passes through. Out of the two or three signs, one will be most suitable for your goals. Time your activity to take place within that period.

The *Old Farmer's Almanac* suggests the following activities be done while the moon is influenced by the associated signs:

- **Plant, Transplant, or Graft:** when the moon is in Cancer, Scorpio, Pisces, or Taurus
- **Harvest:** when the moon is in Aries, Leo, Sagittarius, Gemini, or Aquarius
- **Build/Fix Fences or Garden Beds:** when the moon is in Capricorn
- **Control Insect Pests, Plow, or Weed:** when the moon is in Aries, Leo, Sagittarius, Gemini, or Aquarius
- **Prune:** when the moon is in Aries, Leo, or Sagittarius

MOON PHASES

A lot of traditional gardening is done by moon phase. Gardening by the moon posits that the moon exerts force on plants, the way it exerts force on the tides. When gardening according to the lunar cycle, you will want to be aware of the two main parts of the cycle: the waxing or increasing half, and the waning or decreasing half.

The rule is as follows: Plant fruit and vegetables that bear above ground when the moon is waxing. Annuals should also be planted in this half of the lunar cycle. Plant bulbs, root crops, and perennials in the second half of the lunar cycle. The idea behind this is that as moonlight increases during the night hours, so does the moon's energy, and the plants touched by it are encouraged to grow. As the hours of moonlight decrease, the growing energy shifts to under the ground, benefiting roots, tubers, and bulbs. Likewise, harvest fruit and vegetables that grow above ground in the waxing phase close to when the moon is full, and harvest roots and tubers in the waning phase, closer to the dark moon.

For more on working with the energy of moon phases in your garden, see the next section, as well as Chapter 9.

Moon Gardens

You can choose to plant your entire garden focusing on the moon (a moon phase garden can feature a broad cross-section of plants; see the next section) or designate a small section of your gardening space to devote to the moon in one of the following ways:

- Create a garden evoking moon energy by planting plants that are associated with the moon or that carry energies sympathetic to the moon.
- Create a garden based on moon phases. Such a garden doesn't necessarily have to have moon-related plants in it; plants that resonate with increasing/decreasing styles of magic to different degrees will work just fine.
- Make a garden to enjoy at night. You may choose to do this because you're at work all day, and your only time to enjoy the garden is in the evening.

PLANTS ASSOCIATED WITH THE MOON

The moon itself has plants associated with it, just as the other celestial bodies do. Lunar herbs are generally characterized as cool and moist. They carry feminine energy (yin energy, if you like to think of energy in terms of yin and yang). Here are plants associated with the moon.

- Aloe
- Anise
- Blue lotus
- Chickweed
- Clary sage
- Iris (flower)/Orris (root)
- Ginger
- Ginseng
- Hibiscus
- Milk thistle
- Passionflower
- Poppy
- Rose
- Watercress
- Yerba santa

MOON PHASE GARDEN

A moon phase garden features plants that resonate with increasing/waxing and decreasing/waning styles of magic.

To create a moon phase garden you'll need to:

1. Mark out zones and allocate a moon phase to each: New, waxing, waxing gibbous, full, waning gibbous, waning, and dark.
2. Evaluate the energies of the plants you are interested in working with, check traditional associations, and assign each plant to a zone.
3. Create a blessing ritual to dedicate each zone, to be done during the associated moon phase. This will turn out to be about one ritual every four days or so.

When working magic, if you can't schedule it during the appropriate moon phase, do your work next to the appropriate zone in the garden and draw on that phase-specific energy. (See Chapter 9 for ideas about working magic in your garden.)

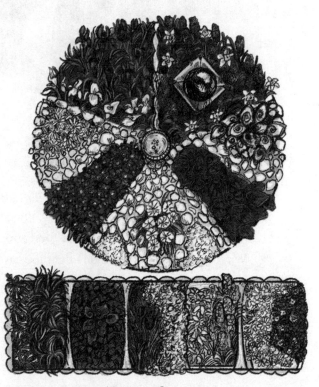

Moon Garden

MOON PHASES AND ASSOCIATED ENERGY

Here's a quick review of moon phases and their associated energies.

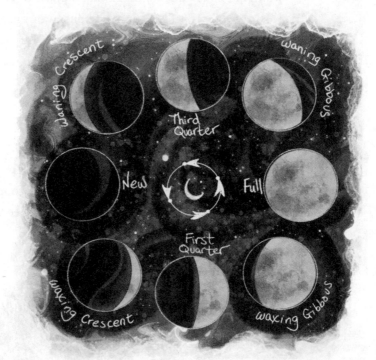

Moon Phases

- **New moon:** The very first sliver of moon seen in the sky, the new moon is appropriately associated with beginnings. It is a good time for setting intentions. It is also a good time to plant in general.
- **Waxing moon:** As the moon's light increases in the sky, the lunar energy shifts to attraction, expansion, and growth. Work on ongoing projects that need support in their development. Prosperity, creativity, and learning are all areas to work on during the waxing moon.
- **Full moon:** This is the energy everyone reaches for, assuming it's the best for whatever they're doing. And in general, the full moon is a great catch-all time to power your magical work. It is about

fruition, success, and culmination. It is an excellent time to harvest plants. The full moon is excellent for blessings and healing work.

- **Waning moon:** As the moon's light decreases, its energy turns to reducing or banishing things. Areas of correspondence sensitive to this energy include healing where the focus is on removing something, minimizing opposition, and overcoming obstacles. It is also a good time for reducing stress and evening out overactivity.
- **Dark moon:** Dark moon energy is good for introspection, preparation for future work, and nourishing your spirit. Quiet, restorative self-care is a good thing to work on at this time. Think of the dark moon as a winter period, where the earth rests and rejuvenates.

A Garden to Enjoy at Night

If you choose to plant a garden to enjoy at night, plants that flower from late afternoon into the night and have a pale appearance are the key things to look for. Moon gardens generally have pale flowers or foliage in order to really stand out at night, whether the moon is out or not.

Many night-blooming plants have ephemeral flowers. They're delicate, and bloom for only a night or so. This adds to their magic, and their romance. It doesn't impact their magical energy.

In deciding where to make your moon garden, choose a location that you'll be able to access at night. This doesn't necessarily have to require going outside; it means positioning your garden where it can be easily enjoyed. You might want to see it through a window where you relax at night, for example. The location also should be in a place that receives moonlight. If this is impossible because of your physical situation (if you're in the Northern Hemisphere, you might be in an apartment that faces north, for example), make sure you have artificial illumination for your moon garden in order to take advantage of the sight.

Not many entire genus groups of plants are classified as night-blooming; generally it's a specific plant or two within the larger genus. The following list suggests a selection of night-blooming plants that you could include in your moon garden.

Casa Blanca Oriental Lily

Lilium orientalis 'Casa Blanca'

The white flowers have an intense fragrance that can be enjoyed at night.

Flowering Tobacco

Nicotiana spp.

Trumpet-shaped florets in a wide variety of colors; *Nicotiana alata* is one of the most fragrant varieties.

Easter Lily Cactus

Echinopsis oxygona

Striking white, fragrant blossoms open up for a night, then begin to wither the next day.

Four O'Clocks

Mirabilis jalapa

Four o'clocks open their bright blooms in the afternoon.

Evening Primrose

Oenothera biennis, Oenothera pallida

Pale blooms open in the evening and close again the next morning.

Gardenia

Gardenia augusta, gardenia jasminoides

Gardenias have a luxurious evening scent and pale flowers.

Moonflower

Ipomoea alba

Moonflowers are medium size, highly scented, bright white flowers.

Night-Blooming Jasmine

Cestrum nocturnum

Tiny flowers, but at night their scent spreads widely.

Night Phlox

Zaluzianskya capensis

Small purple buds that open to white, the plant grows to about a foot, making it ideal for the front of a border.

Rain Lily

Zephyranthes drummondii

Rain lilies open fragrant blooms after a summer rain; this species is also nocturnal.

Tuberose

Polianthes tuberosa

Tall spikes of white flowers that open at night when its fragrance intensifies.

Yucca

Yucca spp.

Creamy-white sweetly scented flower stalks that last much of the summer.

For a website that can help you with moon-related information, visit https://lunarium.co.

Any kind of white or pale flowers can be included in a moon garden. Think of petunias, clematis vines, sweet alyssum, daffodils, tulips, snapdragons, iris, roses, and dahlias. If you choose an assortment of flowers that bloom from early spring to late summer, you'll always have white blooms. If you live in a growing zone that allows for flowers year-round, plan the flowering schedule accordingly. Plants with light-colored foliage to use in your moon garden could include:

- Silver mound artemisia (*Artemisia schmidtiana 'Silver Mound'*)
- Dusty miller (*Senecio cineraria*)
- Lamb's ears (*Stachys byzantina*)
- Licorice (*Helichrysum petiolare*)
- Japanese painted fern (*Athyrium niponicum 'pictum'*)
- Snow-in-summer (*Cerastium tomentosum*)
- Wooly thyme (*Thymus pseudolanuginosus*)

Adding Decor to a Moon Garden

Decor is a beautiful way to enhance your enjoyment of your moon garden. It adds a magical feeling and provides you with an opportunity to further shape the energy of your garden space. You can decorate your garden however you like, but if you want to enhance the silvery, pale aspect of a moon garden, think about these decorative options:

- Fairy lights.
- Gazing ball: polished metal, mirror finish, or glass will glow at night.
- Pale stones to draw the eye to borders, or larger rocks among the plants.
- Solar lights arranged with plants you want to spotlight.
- Water feature: A stone basin or birdbath can be lovely, as it will reflect light at night. If you find the sound of water relaxing, add a small fountain; put it on a timer or switch it on manually.

SOLAR GARDENS

Lunar-themed gardens are lovely, but solar gardens are powerful in a different way. You could argue that all gardens are solar in a way because they all need sunlight to grow, but here we mean a garden of plants specifically linked to the sun. If you live in a place where it's overcast or has periods in the year where you see minimal hours of sunlight for whatever reason, consider planting a solar garden to draw on the solar-associated energy. You might choose to divide your space and plant both a solar garden and a lunar garden, for balance.

Elemental Gardens

Gardens draw on all four elements. They require:

- Earth to grow in
- Water to nourish them
- The warmth of the sun to support their growth
- Air to source carbon dioxide

In magic, we use the four elements as well. If you are a green witch who likes working with elemental energy and magic, elemental gardens may be an interesting theme to pursue.

Every plant has a classical association with one of the four elements. In older sources, sometimes it's based on the plant's appearance, and sometimes it's based on the plant's medical effects or uses. More modern classifications look at the type of magic the plant is generally used for, as well as taking older associations into account. You will find some lists that assign a plant to a different element than other lists, and that's fine.

If it feels odd to think of plant magic as associated with anything other than the element of earth, think about using stones and crystals. Those are also earth-sources, but we don't think of them as solely associated with the element of earth.

Ideally, you should be interacting with these plants (alive or dried samples) and assigning a personal elemental correspondence for them, as well as your own personal magical correspondences. Published lists are a good place to start, but your personal experiences and interactions should always take precedence.

Elemental Garden

When working with elemental magic, there are two basic ideas. The first is to add missing energy to balance out the lack of something. The second is to invoke the energy of the element to initiate active change in accordance with your need.

For example, you may sense that a room tends to be difficult to concentrate in when you study. After evaluating the energy of the space, you may decide it lacks air-associated energy. To add air energy to offset

If you want to honor the four elements in your garden in a different way, include physical representations of them. A small water feature or birdbath can represent water. A fire bowl, pit, or lantern can represent fire. A statue or specially selected stone can represent earth. Air can be evoked by wind chimes, flags, or pinwheels. For a more detailed exploration of garden decor, see Chapter 7.

the lack of focus, you might choose to use plants associated with air, such as lemongrass, sage, or peppermint.

Perhaps you might be putting together a spell for purification. In an elemental context, you might reach for plants associated with water and fire, and specifically draw upon those energies to help achieve your goal.

Unless you're looking to correct an energy imbalance in the physical location of your garden, you're most likely going to want to plant a balanced garden, with equal representations of all four elements. You can plan four separate zones and focus on grouping plants associated with the same elements together, or you can mix them, keeping track in your plans of how many plants you have representing each element.

If you sense an imbalance in your garden location and wish to design your garden to help address that imbalance, include more of the plants associated with the element that is lacking.

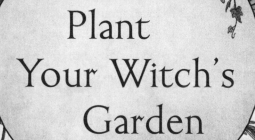

Chapter 4

Plant Your Witch's Garden

Indoors, Outdoors: What and Where

There is flexibility in all forms of gardening, and there are different combinations that will appeal to different witches. The level of complexity will depend on your magical goals. For example, if your goal is to curate a specific kind of energy in a room, your approach will be different from someone who is planning to grow vegetables indoors for food.

While Chapters 2 and 3 led you through designing and planning your garden, this chapter will focus on the places where you can create a garden. Chapter 6 will examine the individual plants and their magical properties, but for now let's focus on breaking down your options for creating gardens in the different places available to you, and what plants do well in each of the places examined. The first half of this chapter will look at various ways to incorporate gardening and working with plants indoors. The second half of this chapter will look at gardening outdoors, be it in containers or in a yard. Read on for insight into different methods of gardening indoors and out.

Indoors and Houseplants

If you don't have an outdoor space—or even if you do, and you want to bring gardening indoors—you have plenty of options!

COMMON HOUSEPLANTS

We tend to not think of houseplants as magical. This is ridiculous, as they're a part of the energy of a home. As witches, we're keenly aware that everything impacts and affects the energy in our living space, and many of us already use plants in some way to influence and shape the feeling in a room or rooms. You may already have common houseplants, so let's take a look at what kind of energies they can carry.

Aspidistra

Aspidistra elatior

Use its energy for commitment, slow and steady work.

Sometimes called cast-iron plants, *Aspidistra elatior* are popular houseplants. They thrive in bright, but not direct, light, and prefer an evenly watered, moist soil. During the growing season, feed them with a controlled-release fertilizer or liquid fertilizer. These are known as tough plants that can withstand a wide range of conditions.

Ferns

Ferns dispel negativity, can be used to cleanse and purify the room, and enhance mental focus.

There are dozens of kinds of ferns, but the most popular to grow indoors include the Boston ferns, or *Nephrolepis exaltata*. Ferns appreciate mild to cool temperatures and thrive in humid rooms and indirect light. If your growing area is arid or dry, mist your ferns regularly, put them in a tray with pebbles and water, or group them with other plants to increase humidity. Feed your ferns in spring and keep them well watered.

Ivy

Ivy traditionally carries energies associated with loyalty, but can also be used for fertility and protection.

Grape ivy (*Cissus rhombifolia*) is a pretty green plant that climbs, but some varieties also have a tendency to be thick and mound-like. It's a good choice if you want ivy, but I have ended up with anemic or spindly examples in the past. Grape ivy is a member of the grape family and does well as a hanging plant. Like other ivies, grape ivy likes cooler temperatures (between about 62 and 82 degrees F), and it does best in medium light. Water your grape ivy regularly, but let it dry between waterings. A waterlogged ivy will decline and eventually die.

Ivy

Ivy traditionally carries energies associated with loyalty, but can also be used for fertility and protection.

English ivy (*Hedera helix*) can be invasive and hard to control outdoors, but inside it can be managed easier in hanging baskets. English ivy thrives in cooler temperatures and has somewhat more specific needs than some other popular houseplants. English ivy likes bright light and can tolerate some direct sun, but it will shrivel in dark corners. Similarly, English ivy is sensitive to being overwatered, but it likes relatively high humidity, so mist your ivy frequently, but be careful not to overwater it.

Norfolk Island Pine

Araucaria heterophylla

Magically, like other conifers, Norfolk Island pines represent life, and carry purification and cleansing energy.

Often found in December during the festive season, these plants are touted as alternatives to full-sized harvested pines for indoor celebrations. They make great houseplants year-round, though. Norfolk pines aren't true pines at all; they're tropical plants and need heat, humidity, and light.

Philodendron

Philodendron spp.

Philodendrons are excellent at cleaning air, and magically can be used for cleansing and lifting negative or stagnant energy.

There are over 450 species of philodendron, including climbing and non-climbing varieties. They are rewarding to keep, as they grow quickly and are pretty hardy, and they propagate well via cuttings placed in water. They prefer partial sunlight and humidity like that of their tropical origins, along with plenty of water (and good drainage). The white sap of philodendrons is mildly caustic, so wear gloves when you're handling plant cuttings.

Pothos

Epipremnum aureum

Magically, pothos is good at cleansing energy and bringing a lighter, airier feel to the energy of a space.

The pothos tolerates a variety of light conditions and can be propagated in either water or soil; indeed, pothos will live happily in water. Pothos vines are among the easiest houseplants to grow—they endure uneven watering for long periods before dropping leaves. They don't like cold drafts for long, however. If you have cats and dogs, be aware that the pothos vine is toxic to your animals. A well-cared-for pothos vine quickly climbs a moss pole or cascades from a hanging basket as a beautiful decorative plant.

Schefflera

Schefflera spp.

Use the schefflera for grounding energy.

Sometimes called umbrella plant for how the leaf stems grow out from the central spoke, similar to the ribs of an umbrella. Another hardy indoor plant, the schefflera can get quite large, so you might have to prune your schefflera to keep it manageable. Schefflera appreciate medium light but can tolerate some direct morning or afternoon light, and they like regular, even watering. Toxic.

Spider Plant

Chlorophytum comosum

Use spider plants for fertility or abundance energy.

Spider plants are one of the most popular houseplants for a simple reason: They are very tough and beautiful. Well-grown plants send out little plantlets on arching stems that resemble spiders. Spider plants like medium light and regular watering and feeding. They are widely tolerant, however, of mistakes with watering, so this is a great plant for beginning gardeners or in rooms where it seems nothing else will grow.

Indoor Growing Racks

Indoor grow systems use space efficiently by stacking wire shelving to create a rack-like stand. Designed for seed starting, these systems often come with fittings for lights that can be set on a timer for a reliable, consistent lighting schedule. Grow racks have use beyond starting seeds, however! If you want to grow things that won't do well outside in your hardiness zone, or you want to have all your plants gathered in one area for ease of tending them, then an indoor grow rack may be your answer.

Self-contained grow tents take your control even further, enabling you to create an almost entirely different climate with a completely enclosed tent; these include lights, fans, and filters that allow you to control the temperature, humidity, and light cycles inside the tent.

Clear covers can be used on grow racks, enabling you to better control the climate inside them, as in a greenhouse. These covers protect the plants inside, while allowing you to see and appreciate the plants. They can generally be opened with a zipper, and the sides folded back to allow you to tend the plants inside. Decorating these covers with sigils or art, or charms and spell bags designed for protection, abundance, health, and growth is a great idea. Your imagination is the limit.

Multiple Mini Garden Areas

There is no rule that says houseplants have to be in the same place. In fact, different plants with different growing requirements will do better in different places—think in front of windows, in humid areas, in drier places, in dimmer places, and so forth. You may also have other conditions that dictate what plants you can have and where you put them: sensitivities, pets that can damage or eat plants, cold drafts, and so forth. Taking these things into account, you can look at the different areas of your living space and make decisions regarding the plants you can safely have in your home, and that will suit the conditions your space offers. If you're new to indoor gardening, choose plants that are time tested and already known for being easier to grow inside. This list includes pothos vines, sword plants, spider plants, and many of the most popular and common houseplants.

Alternative Indoor Gardens

Lush potted plants are one way of cultivating an indoor garden space, but sometimes that option is not accessible. If you want living green things in your home but can't have pots of them for whatever reason, you have several alternative possibilities. Remember that, in general, a plant needs just three things: soil, water, and light.

TERRARIUMS

A terrarium is a great option for small-space gardening. Terrariums have been used by indoor gardeners for centuries. Closed terrariums are totally enclosed systems that provide a growing medium (like soil), light, and water. Old aquariums make excellent terrariums, as they are made from glass and already watertight. A well-balanced closed terrarium will require little additional maintenance once you've set it up and planted it. One of the keys to a successful closed terrarium is to enable the right conditions for the required levels of humidity. Ideally, a closed terrarium will operate like a little self-contained ecosystem, with water being given off from plants to create humidity and then dripping back down into the soil just like rain. An established closed terrarium needs very little ongoing maintenance—because it's a closed system, you don't need to water regularly.

When you're choosing plants for a closed terrarium, pick plants that thrive on humidity. Good options include many kinds of beautiful mosses, small ferns like artillery ferns, and attractive small foliage plants like polka dot

Of paramount importance is the safety of children and pets. Research your choices carefully for toxicity. If you choose to grow a plant that is toxic in some way to members of your household, consider its placement carefully. Putting something in a hanging planter may keep a plant out of the reach of children, for example, but not a particularly dexterous cat.

plants (*Hypoestes phyllostachya*). With a little imagination, you can also transform your enclosed terrarium into a tiny jewel garden, with beautiful rocks, small statues, and other totems.

If a closed terrarium sounds too difficult, you can also plant an open terrarium. These miniature gardens are open to the air, so there is no lid to trap moisture and create a small water cycle. These terrariums will require regular watering just like other container plants, and the range of plants you can grow in an open terrarium is limited only by the size of your container.

Closed Terrarium   *Open Terrarium*

Finally, you can create a hybrid terrarium with a bottle or other narrow-necked container. These bottle gardens aren't completely closed, so their humidity levels do not have to be as carefully calibrated as with a closed terrarium (but they require that you pay attention to regular and careful watering). Bottle gardens can create a great element of surprise, as you can sprinkle seeds into the container and watch as the garden fills in.

AQUATIC PLANTS

If you have an aquarium or fish tank, consider live plants. In recent years, many people have started growing jewel-like aquatic freshwater gardens in aquariums—sometimes even without fish! If it seems intimidating to grow freshwater plants, the key is to start small and plan it out carefully.

In general, aquatic plants fall into one of the following categories:

- **Foreground plants:** Low and spreading plants that can form a vibrant green carpet.
- **Midground plants:** Slightly taller and perfect for planting along the sides or middle of your tank as specimens.
- **Background plants:** Taller and larger plants that form the backdrop against which your fish, aquarium decorations, and smaller plants will shine.

As you're planning your aquarium, make sure you are providing the right growing environment. Just like their terrestrial cousins, aquatic plants need a soil (or substrate) to grow into. Specially formulated soils for aquariums can make your job much easier by providing a perfect substrate—regular aquarium gravel isn't a good choice for most aquatic plants. You'll also need to supply a full-spectrum light. The good news is that the same light your fish enjoy will also be good for your plants in most cases.

Aquarium

Once you've got your lights and substrate set up, you have many options to choose from when planting. Consider starting out with easier plants like Java moss, water wisteria, Amazon sword, Java fern, and *Anubias*. If you have questions, your local aquarium store is a great source of information.

SUCCULENTS

Succulents are plants with fleshy parts that can store water. These parts can be leaves, the stems, or the roots. Common succulents include jade plants, aloe vera, snake plants, and agave.

Succulents are rewarding in that they're usually happy to have sips of water every couple of weeks. They're not fond of extremes; too much water and they'll rot, too little and their roots and fleshy parts will dry up. Succulents are drought tolerant but not drought resistant. That means they do need water on a regular basis, just less frequently than other houseplants. Water them when the soil dries out, then wait for it to dry out again. Make sure they have adequate drainage. They do need sunlight too. At the same time, direct sunlight can be too aggressive for them. Indirect light is a good compromise.

Succulents

Succulents are good for reminding you that moderation in all things and a balanced approach are both very important. A succulent is designed by nature to conserve water in its fleshy parts, allowing it to deal with extended dry periods. If you have difficulty with overflowing emotional responses to situations or events, perhaps working with succulents could be beneficial. Feeling your emotions is valuable; being unable to function clearly because you are overwhelmed by emotion, or feeling drained because you feel so deeply, is a hindrance. Protecting your emotional self is a form of self-defense and protection. Meditate, reach out to the plant spirit (see Chapters 1 and 9), and ask for its guidance in how to balance your responses and deepest feelings in a beneficial, safe way.

CACTI

Cacti are one of the most popular types of succulents (but not all succulents are cacti).

Cacti

Cacti usually have thickened, fleshy parts designed to store water against drought conditions. These parts are usually the stems. Instead of leaves, cacti usually have spines, which help filter the light and reduce the airflow around the plant, with the added benefit of protecting the plant from plant-eating predators. Some species of cacti, like the Christmas cactus, feature beautiful flowers, while others are known for their architectural and beautiful structure. Some of the most popular indoor cacti include members of the prickly pear family, the rat tail cactus, the saguaro or barrel cactus, and the old lady cactus. It's tempting to think of cacti as exclusively desert plants that thrive in very hot, arid conditions—and this is true for some cacti, but not all of them. In general, provide your cacti with a very fast-draining soil, medium to bright light, and warmth. It's a misconception to think cacti never need water. In fact, your cacti will appreciate being moistened regularly, as long as you let all the water drain out of the soil between waterings. Cacti can tolerate regular watering, but will suffer if they are allowed to sit in water or the soil becomes waterlogged.

A cactus suggests working alone, preserving energy. Cacti are often drawn on in protection magic as well, due to the presence of spines. They make good anchors for magical wards, semi-permanent defensive shields around a location. Cacti can also represent endurance in magical work.

A common houseplant is the Christmas cactus. It's not an arid cactus but a tropical one.

Feng shui sees cacti as harmful to the calm flow of energy, but you can use that to break up persistent negative or unwanted energy. A cactus's spiky presence will shred up this type of energy. Feng shui also sees the cactus as a symbol of protecting wealth, so you can use them in prosperity magic.

Cacti can be used to either repel or protect. It's up to you to decide which way to code your cactus (or cacti; there's no rule against using multiple cacti for different goals). Be mindful of where you place them, and how they can affect the energy of the area around them.

AIR PLANTS

Air plants don't need soil. They grow on things instead of in earth (the word for a plant like this is *epiphyte*); their roots are used to grip objects rather than drawing nutrients from the soil. Instead, their leaves draw moisture from the air to nourish the plant. Air plants can grow on many surfaces, including cork, wood mounts, stone, and tree fern slabs, and they can even simply hang in midair.

Some of the most popular air plants are in the *Tillandsia* genus. These delicate and beautiful spiky little plants are often grown hanging in glass globes, offering a staggering array of vibrant colors like purple and red and thriving with simple misting. Bromeliads are another common and beautiful type of air plant. Although they are often sold potted in soil, bromeliads can be grown mounted on driftwood or tree fern. Finally, some of the best-known air plants are orchids. Although there are tens of thousands of types of orchids, by far the most popular are all epiphytes that grow naturally mounted on trees or stones. While growing orchids as air plants requires patience and some experience, it's possible even in most homes to grow beautiful and blooming orchids.

Orchid

The care of your air plants will depend on what type of air plant it is, but there are certain similarities among all of them. Air plants thrive on the right mix of light, moisture, airflow, and temperature. Most of them appreciate regular watering, usually with a mister or spray bottle. Bromeliads, which usually have a central "cup" that catches water, need only to be filled with water whenever the level is low. Orchids like regular watering with a period of "hard drying" between watering to prevent mold and fungus from attacking your plant. While these plants may require some patience to master growing, air plants are some of the most exotic and beautiful plants in the world. Air plants can be good sources of energy for people looking to incorporate more air energy into their environment or workings.

Winter Gardening

Are you restless during the winter months? Living in a climate where outdoor gardening has a definite time limit can make you lonely for green things during the icy stretch when your garden outdoors is dreaming deep under a thick blanket of snow. Designing an indoor garden space can help.

There are a few things to keep in mind. Depending on your location, winter light can be too weak on its own even if you have large windows; luckily, grow lights can shore that up. Grow lights can supplement the natural lighting, or even replace it if you choose to work in a room with small windows or that faces north, for example. Flooring also needs to be considered. Carpeting and wood can be damaged by indoor gardening. Also, there needs to be decent airflow. If the room you're working in doesn't have great flow, you can use a ceiling or floor fan. Winters can be dry due to indoor heating, but a small humidifier can help remedy that.

Other ways to pass the winter months indoors can be enjoyable too. For help planning next year's garden, read gardening magazines, pore through seed catalogs, sketch different layouts, and review what worked well and what didn't this past year.

Vegetables from Kitchen Waste

Growing your vegetables from kitchen waste is a great way to incorporate gardening indoors. It can be done fully indoors or as a windowsill garden. Growing vegetables from kitchen scraps reduces food waste, can save you money, and allows you the experience of both growing things and eating them. It's much easier than you might think. It does require you to pay attention and respond to the plant's needs, like changing the water daily or misting it. (Of course, if your focus is elsewhere, programming reminders for yourself isn't cheating. I promise.)

LEAFY HEAD VEGETABLES

Leafy head vegetables include things like lettuces (especially romaine), celery, bok choy, and cabbage. To grow these from scraps, first cut off the base (making sure you have about one inch of the plant) and set it in a shallow dish of some kind. Add about a half inch of water and set the dish in a sunny place. Replace the water every day or two. These can be grown year-round on a windowsill, either in water or transferred to soil once the roots show. If you plant it, cover the roots and base with earth, but leave the top free. Leafy greens like these can also be grown by placing a few leaves in a glass with a bit of water at the bottom. Mist them every 1–2 days and change the water every couple of days.

BULB VEGETABLES

Bulb vegetables include green onions, leeks, fennel, and shallots. For these, cut one inch off the root end. Place it root end down in a half inch of water.

It takes about a week or two to grow a new green onion. You can snip off what you need and leave the white base to keep growing. Change the water every couple of days.

A small glass works better than a dish for these. Garlic and onions, while also bulb vegetables, need slightly different techniques to grow. For garlic, take a clove and plant it root downward in potting soil. Place the container in an area with good light. When new shoots begin to grow up out of the bulb, trim them off and allow the plant to focus its growing energy in the bulb. Regular bulb onions don't grow well in water; they prefer to be planted directly into potting soil or your garden. Take your one inch of root end and plant it in soil, root base down, and leave the cut end exposed.

ROOT VEGETABLES

Root vegetables include things like turnips, beets, carrots, and parsnips. With root vegetables, the root gets eaten, and the top where leaves grew gets discarded. You won't be able to regrow a root from the top scrap, but you can sprout new leaves, which can be fed to pets, such as rabbits, or snipped off and added to salads or stir-fries. Cut off the top of the root vegetable, leaving about a half inch attached, and set it cut side down in a half inch of water in a shallow dish. Replace the water regularly.

Ginger, though also a root vegetable, requires a different technique. To grow new ginger, plant a small piece of the ginger root in potting soil, with the smaller end facing up.

HERBS

In general, you can place a stem of an herb (about four inches long, with at least one growing node submerged) in a glass of water, and place it somewhere well lit, but not in direct sunlight. When the roots are a couple of inches long, transplant the herb into potting soil.

Windowsill and Window Box Gardens

Windowsill and window box gardens are terrific for things like herbs. They're often found in kitchens, where they're within reach when needed for cooking. If you don't have a lot of space indoors, a windowsill or window boxes can offer you some flexibility.

If you have more than one window, you can plan themed boxes: one designed to attract prosperity, one with plants for protection, and so forth. If you can only have one box, choose plants that cover a range of purposes.

WINDOW BOXES

Often used for ornamental purposes, window boxes can provide so much more than just decoration. Window boxes outside offer the opportunity to grow plants that aren't necessarily as happy inside. They're designed to be easily accessed from the open window, allowing you to care for any plants growing in them. Choose plants that have similar watering, light, and soil requirements when planning a window box. Some smaller vegetables will grow perfectly well in a window box.

There are a few things to keep in mind when gardening with window boxes. First, they're not very large, so they dry out quickly. Check the soil regularly to make sure it stays moist enough for the plants you're growing. When hanging them, choose brackets that space the box away from the wall, so water doesn't get trapped between the two surfaces, which can damage the exterior of the wall. Look for brackets that are long, or position them so that the upper edge of the box hangs below the bottom of the window; this allows taller plants to have room to grow without blocking the view, and it's especially important if your window opens outward. And finally, use light potting soil, not topsoil; one of the keys to working with window boxes is keeping the box as light as possible.

WINDOWSILL GARDENS

An easy, inexpensive way to involve plants in your daily life, windowsill gardens are as simple as placing small pots or containers along your windowsill. When choosing windows for this kind of gardening, look for a bright, sunny window (indirect light is often fine, as long as there's a good amount). Bright sunlight in winter is especially important, but it doesn't have to be direct sunlight. You'll want to choose plants that can tolerate inconsistent or fluctuating light. Herbs and leafy greens are good for this. Rotate the positions of the plants and which side faces the window regularly.

Remember that the containers you choose should have drainage. Group smaller containers together on a narrow tray to catch drips and spills.

It's important that the windowsill you choose have a relatively consistent temperature, so the plants won't be subjected to the stress of having to adjust to fluctuations. If you live in a climate that gets very cold, look for plants that will be hardy enough to handle the cold radiating from the glass of the window. Kitchen windowsills by a sink are particularly good for this type of garden. The warm humidity from your sink will bathe the plants, making it possible to grow even challenging tropical plants like anthurium.

If you don't have a window with enough of a sill to safely set things on and an outdoor window box is impossible for whatever reason, there are a couple of fairly simply DIY ways to create more shelf space inside in front of your window.

Windowsill Sprout Magic

If you have a windowsill garden or if everything is covered with snow where you are, here's a bit of magic that you can perform indoors. This spell uses the physical act of growing to infuse the plant with your magical goal. This version calls for broccoli sprouts, but you can use any seed (look up the proportions and the edibility of the seeds you intend to use). This spell can also be adapted to microgreens. The recipe yields about 3 cups broccoli sprouts. Sprouts can be eaten any time after sprouting begins, but generally people prefer them when they are an inch or two long.

You'll Need: 3 tablespoons broccoli seeds • 1-quart Mason jar (wide mouth) • Water • Scissors • Cheesecloth • Pen or pencil • Elastic band • Fine sieve • Large bowl

1 Put the seeds in the jar. Cover the seeds with cool water.

2 Cut a circle of cheesecloth 1½ times the diameter of the mouth of the jar. With the pen or pencil, draw a rune or symbol that you associate with your magical goal onto the circle of cheesecloth. If you prefer, you can write out a spell on the cloth. Set the cheesecloth over the mouth of the jar and secure it with the elastic band. Leave the seeds to soak for 8 hours.

3 Remove the cheesecloth and place the sieve over the mouth of the jar. Invert the jar and allow the water to drain out. Revert the jar and sieve and allow the seeds to fall to the bottom of the jar again. Tap the sieve against the top of the jar to loosen any stubborn seeds.

4 Add more cool water to the jar, swirl it around to rinse the seeds, and drain it again. Remove as much water as possible. Replace the cheesecloth. Set the jar upside down at an angle in the bowl to allow water to drain out and air to circulate.

5 Rinse the seeds twice a day. Each time you rinse and drain, empower the sprouts with your magical goal or repeat the written spell. The seeds will sprout in a few days. As they sprout, the shoots become empowered with your magical goal.

6 Rinse the sprouts a final time, spread them on a kitchen towel (cloth or paper) and pat them dry. Consume them in some way—part of a salad, stir-fry, sandwich—and focus on internalizing the magic. Wash the cloth or compost it.

A hanging shelf suspended in front of the window is one thing you might consider. You will need a simple wooden board with large eye-bolts or screws set into each corner; two lengths of rope or cord, each twice the distance from the ceiling to where you want your board to be (plus extra for tying knots and running the cord across the narrow end of the board); and sturdy hooks set into the ceiling spaced apart the length of the board. Run each piece of cord through the two eye-bolts across a short end of the board, then tie the ends of each into a loop. Hang each loop from a ceiling hook. Retie the knots to adjust the height as desired.

Alternatively, a board hung in front of a window from a sturdy curtain rod or hooks set in the wall above or to the sides of the window can create a hanging shelf, or you can place brackets or shelf supports beneath your window and lay your board across those. Use logic when setting up plants on a board or shelf like this; large ceramic pots belong somewhere sturdier. Hanging shelves like this are great for starting cuttings, small herbs, or growing vegetable scraps in water (see earlier in this chapter). Remember when you're planting any type of shelf garden to plan for drainage—simple drainage trays to catch water can prevent a lot of damage. If you need to raise the humidity, you can place your containers in larger trays with pebbles and water. The evaporating water will raise the humidity around your plants.

Container Gardening

Container gardening is the practice of growing plants in containers, either inside or outside. This makes it easier to take advantage of your indoor spaces and can help you organize an outdoor garden or work with other outdoor places like a balcony or pool area. Container gardening also allows people with limited mobility to garden, as working with containers is much easier than roaming around a plot of land. As a bonus, you can place containers on low tables or another sort of base to bring all the plants to a level comfortable for you to work with. Suspended baskets also qualify as container gardening and can make use of space even if the floor or ground is occupied.

Beyond these basics, there's no limit to what you can grow in containers. Vegetables like tomatoes, peppers, cucumbers, broccoli, and many others thrive in containers. If you're interested in flowers, you can create dramatic displays of bright blooms combined with trailing plants like vines for mixed containers. If you're growing outside, include pollinator-friendly options like hyssop, cosmos, lavender, and coneflower to attract bees, butterflies, and even hummingbirds to your container garden.

No matter your reasons for gardening in containers—lack of space, lack of open land, mobility issues, or simply preference—there are some powerful advantages to containers. First, containers make it much easier to guarantee that your plants are getting exactly the right nutrients they need and that they are growing in high-quality potting media. (Never use regular garden soil in a container, as it's too heavy; instead use a potting soil designed for containers.) Also, because they can be located anywhere, containers make it possible to bring your garden onto your deck or patio, your balcony, or even a covered pool area. This can be especially helpful if you have issues like deer that attack your plants.

In addition to these advantages, container gardening can present unique challenges. To ensure success, keep a few important points in mind. First, everything your plant needs to grow must be provided in the container, especially water. In the ground, a thirsty plant can send out longer roots. In a container, an underwatered plant will simply die, so you'll have to make sure you can provide regular water. Alternatively, you can experiment with self-watering systems that are designed to provide the exact amount of water a plant needs. Also, as tempting as it might be, it's usually not a good idea to reuse container soil from year to year. Container potting media is usually made from composted peat moss that decomposes and compresses over time. In general, you should aim to repot or refresh your container soil every year. Finally, it's especially important to feed your container plants with a high-quality fertilizer because they won't be able to draw nutrients from the ground.

WALL GARDENS

A wall garden is a specialized type of container garden with containers mounted on a wall to create a cascading effect. These can work indoors or outdoors, but if you're growing indoors make sure to pay attention to drainage so you don't damage your floors or the wall. Wall gardens can be created using any type of container as long as it can be securely fastened to the wall. Once you've built your wall garden, you can plant it with flowering annuals, aroids or decorative plants, or especially herbs like basil, thyme, and oregano, which are the perfect size and temperament for wall gardens.

Not just ornamental, hanging baskets can be used to grow vegetables too. Like window boxes, hanging baskets can dry out very quickly, depending on your climate. Keep a close eye on their moisture levels. If your baskets are in a sunny area and require frequent watering, make sure they're low enough for you to access easily, or have a step stool on hand.

Outdoor Gardens

The stereotypical witch's garden is lush and full, with a wide variety of plants and an organic feel to the layout. It's a lovely visual image, but the reality is most of us don't live in a climate that supports that kind of garden.

We have to take our geographic location and climate into account when visualizing our ideal gardens. Sustaining a lush fairy-tale garden in a climate that doesn't support that kind of growing would take an immense amount of time, energy, soil alteration, and water. That's the opposite of working with the land. That's trying to force the land and your plants to do something they're not designed to do. Your outdoor climate will be the ultimate determiner of the range of plants you can grow.

Good places to start for learning about what types of plants will thrive in your environment are your local county extension office, local garden clubs, or even classes. Once you've learned about your local conditions, you can begin to plan your garden. Working outdoors, in the land you also live on, is a very powerful way to stay connected to nature and the earth. Some of the tasks your outdoor garden might require are building raised beds; aerating and loosening soil in preparation for planting; adding compost or other organic material to your local soil to improve it; building structures like trellises for vines and running plants; laying out beds and installing edging; laying irrigation hoses or sprinklers; laying mulch; creating paths; and, of course, adding special features like benches, fountains, and garden art that will make the space uniquely your own.

What if there's a special plant you want to try growing, but it's not ideal for your hardiness zone? There's nothing that says your witch's garden can't exist in several different places. It's easier to control your environment indoors, especially in a grow tent or an enclosed plant rack. Grow what you can outdoors, use containers for vulnerable plants that need more protection and attention, and grow plants that require a careful control of their environment inside.

Your exact garden will depend on what your goal is. If you want to grow a wildflower garden, free-form beds with narrow paths will create the wild, organic look you might want. If you're growing vegetables and herbs, you might want to lay out your garden in a series of clearly defined beds for crops like beans, tomatoes, peppers, carrots, and more. If your soil is full of sand or clay, you might want to create raised beds for your plants. A raised bed is simply an elevated growing bed, usually walled in with wood or even cement blocks and filled in with high-quality topsoil.

If it sounds like the options are unlimited, that's because they pretty much are, but there's no need to be overwhelmed by all the available choices. Just take it slow and be open to the possibilities. Your outdoor garden will be limited only by your own imagination and your growing experience with your unique land. Whether you're growing an herb garden, a catnip patch, a vegetable garden, or a formal topiary garden, every year you are growing outside you will learn more about your environment. Keep a garden journal and note events like the date of your last frost, types of birds and insects you see in your garden, and your watering and feeding schedule. You might be surprised how often you return to your own garden journal to remind yourself about a bit of knowledge you learned in a previous year that will help you become a better, more connected gardener in the future.

Chapter 5

Prepare Your Sacred Space

Gather Your Tools

Every witch has tools they prefer to use, whether it be in ritual, the kitchen, or the garden. If you're taking on gardening as a serious hobby, taking the time to think about the specialized tools you'll need is a good plan. While you don't have to run out and buy a new set of expensive tools, gardening is very hands-on, and there are certain tools that will make your work easier. Why use something that kind of works when the tool that would be more efficient exists? Witchcraft has a time-honored tradition of reusing or recycling, but when it comes to energy being invested in something like a garden, it can make sense to invest in the tools designed for the purpose. The good news is that, depending on your fitness level, budget, and size of your garden, you may not need a huge new shed full of tools or vehicles. People have been gardening for millennia, often with only the most rudimentary tools, so there's no reason to let a "lack" of the latest, most expensive garden gadgets interfere with your plan to grow beautiful plants.

CHOOSING GARDENING TOOLS

Like other tools used in witchcraft, gardening tools are personal. Some you will find essential, while others won't feature in your regular repertoire. Your physical space for gardening also will dictate what you'll need. If your garden is entirely indoors, for example, a rake won't do you much good. You can condense your tool set to smaller handheld versions. Likewise, if you have the opportunity to work with a large amount of land, the bigger tools will be more efficient than the smaller ones. No one wants to use a small hand trowel to turn over an acre of earth.

Following is an overview of common gardening tools.

GLOVES

Gloves are important, especially for outdoor work. You may think you don't need them, but you will inevitably encounter something particularly messy and wish you had a pair, and gripping thick, sharp stems is always easier with them. Gloves can be tricky, however. You want something heavy enough to protect your hands, but light enough to maintain mobility and finger dexterity. Breathable is good—no one enjoys the slimy feeling of hot, sweaty hands inside a stuffy glove, especially when you're trying to hold on to things—and a water-resistant material or coating is also helpful.

PRUNING SHEARS

Pruning shears are used to cut plant matter for various purposes, such as harvesting, trimming, or removing. Look for a set of shears that fits comfortably in your hand. Too big, and your hands will strain, and the snipping motion won't be as efficient.

> For either type of shears, a ratchet-based style will help increase cutting power without straining your hand.

There are two types of shears. Bypass shears feature a sharp blade passing a second sharp surface; these are used to cut live green stems and wood cleanly. Anvil-style shears have a sharp blade meeting a flat surface; these are for cutting dead plant matter, because they crush the drier structure and enable it to be taken off.

GARDEN FORKS

Garden forks generally fall into one of two categories: straight tines or curved tines. A pitchfork's tines have a slight curve, designed to scoop up and toss material, like hay. Straight-tined forks are ideal for digging and loosening up soil.

SPADES AND SHOVELS

These tools are similar in style but serve slightly different purposes. Spades have flat, square-shaped blades used for breaking up roots and ground. Shovels have curved blades with a rounded or pointed tip, used for turning soil. Both can be used for moving soil and digging.

HOES

Hoes have a short, flat blade set perpendicular to the shaft. They are used for stirring and moving the soil around plants to deter weed growth, and to break up clumps in the soil and distribute soil additives.

WEEDER

A weeder is a super useful tool for outdoor gardeners. There are many types, but all feature sharp tines that can dig into soil and lift up weeds by their roots. Long-handled weeders make it possible to clear weeds from your garden beds without bending over as much.

HAND RAKE

The hand rake/fork looks like a miniature weeder. It's typically a handheld three-pronged tool with bent tines, resembling a hand with bent fingers. It's often found in sets with a trowel (see the following). A hand rake is great for mixing fertilizer or soil additives into soil, refreshing the surface and breaking up clumps, and digging holes to plant new things.

HAND TROWEL

A hand trowel is like a miniature handheld shovel or spade. A hand trowel allows you more precise control over the movement of soil, like when digging a hole to plant seedlings. A broad blade trowel moves more dirt, but a narrow one makes it easier to dig in packed earth.

Handles are really important. Unlike ritual tools, gardening tools require sustained physical use, and therefore their comfort in the hand is critical. If the handle is too wide, too short, or at an uncomfortable angle, using it will be awkward at best and painful at worst. Try out various styles to discover what you prefer.

RAKE

A full-sized rake comes in handy for a variety of garden tasks. Springy fan-shaped rakes are used to rake up leaves or cuttings after pruning, or for refreshing grass or ground cover. Straight metal rakes that look like a comb fastened to the end of a long handle are for tilling a large area of soil or sifting rocks or branches from soil.

WATERING TOOLS

Watering tools are essential no matter where your garden is located. Watering cans and buckets transport water from a central source to where it's needed. Hoses and drip systems can carry water steadily and slowly. Indoors, a light watering can with a long spout is useful. Outdoors, a larger, sturdier watering can with a sprinkle spout cap is more efficient. A fine mister can be used for plants that like humidity.

MISCELLANEOUS TOOLS AND SUPPLIES

Here are other tools and supplies that can make gardening easier:

- **Garden tags** or garden stakes identify what is planted where. You may think you'll remember. You won't.
- A **soil tester/meter** can measure the pH level of the soil, light levels, and moisture levels. These are very useful for gardeners who aren't sure what plants will grow best in their soil, what part of their room constitutes diffused light, or what kind of watering frequency specific plants require.
- **Draining trays** are useful, especially for indoor gardens. Fill the tray with small stones and then sit your pots on top. This allows them extra drainage, as well as protecting your furniture from water stains. Draining trays work well in tandem with plant stands.
- **Grow lights** can supplement short daylight hours indoors in winter. If you grow plants inside with a rack or shelf system, a cover for it to keep humidity in can also be useful. It turns your rack into a greenhouse-like environment. Some of the best grow lights available today are LED lights. These relatively inexpensive options don't consume much electricity or put out a lot of heat, so you can grow a variety of plants without complicated equipment like fans or specialized light hoods and ballasts.

The boline is a tool sometimes mentioned in Wicca books. It's a blade that complements the athame, the ceremonial knife used in ritual to direct energy. The athame is sometimes dull on one or both edges to indicate that it is a tool used symbolically, not as a practical blade. The boline, on the other hand, is a sharp blade, often with a white handle to mirror the athame's black one, generally with some kind of curve to the blade. It's specifically used for physical work—for example, harvesting herbs and carving things on candles.

In gardening terminology, this type of curved-blade tool is called a hand sickle. As a garden witch, you can use one if you like. Sickles have a learning curve, however (no pun intended), and your pruning shears are probably more likely to be the appropriate and accessible tool. And there's no rule that says everyday tools can't also be tools used in magic. Green witchcraft is about practicality, after all. We recognize the spiritual in the everyday.

WITCHY TOOLS

There are tools that we use in witchcraft that don't necessarily show up on lists of gardening tools, but they can be handy for garden-related purposes. You might want to include them in your green witch gardening kit.

BROOM

A broom (sometimes called a besom) is a tool used to clear unwanted energy from a space. In a practical path like that of the green witch, your everyday broom might also be used as a spiritual tool. You can extend this to your garden space, using your broom to clear walkways, patios, and stairs, be they indoors or out.

OFFERING DISH

An offering dish of some kind (plate, bowl, or other) to be placed outside as part of a ritual, spell, or honoring is a good idea. If you prefer, you can have a designated bit of ground where you pour or leave your offerings, or use various places in the garden according to your needs.

STANG

The stang is a forked stick, essentially shaped like an uppercase Y. It's a fantastic tool to use in outdoor witchcraft, as it serves as an altar and/or shrine of sorts, able to support charm bags, cords used in cord magic, bundles of herbs for drying, tying strips of cloth, and anything else you can think of. Find one on your property after trees have been pruned, or go for a walk in a public park or wooded area to find branches on the ground and cut one to bring home.

STAFF

The staff is a wand cognate, used to direct energy in ritual. It is also a practical tool, used for drawing symbols or lines on the ground if you're working magic in the garden.

CAULDRON

The cauldron can be used as a container for fire, practical for magical work in the garden. Make sure to set the cauldron on a stone or tile, so the feet or base don't conduct heat into the plants around it. (Take care when working with fire in the garden, as earth can always have bits of roots or vegetable matter in it that can smolder or catch fire.) A cauldron can also be used for potions intended for watering, sprinkling, aspersing the plants, and so forth.

MORTAR AND PESTLE

A mortar and pestle can be useful in preparing herbs and dried plants for spellwork or cooking.

DEDICATING YOUR TOOLS

If you're the kind of witch who likes to dedicate their everyday tools as magical tools, you may want to dedicate your gardening tools. Following is a simple dedication ritual for that purpose. Personalize it as you desire!

RITUAL

Dedicating a Tool

If gardening is a spiritual practice for you, dedicating your tools will help key them into your energy and prepare them for a better sympathetic resonance with your goals. This small ritual can be used for any tool that supports your work in the garden. If you prefer, instead of using a small dish of soil, you can do the ritual outside in your garden space.

You'll Need: Votive candle or tea light in a holder • Matches or lighter • The tool (or tools) • Small dish or glass of water • Small dish of soil

1 Center and ground. Light the candle.

2 Take up the tool. Say,

> *(Name of tool), you are from this moment my partner,*
> *Supporting my work of cultivation, nurturing, and care.*
> *You are an extension of my hands and my will.*
> *Your part in this work is vital.*
> *I dedicate you to the work of tending and uplifting nature.*
> *Welcome to my service.*

Breathe gently on the tool, and say,

> *By air, I dedicate you.*

Pass the tool over the candle flame, and say,

> *By fire, I dedicate you.*

Dip your fingers into the water and shake them onto the tool, and say,

> *By water, I dedicate you.*

Finally, sprinkle the tool with a pinch of earth, or lay it on the ground, and say,

> *By earth, I dedicate you.*

3 Close your eyes and imagine a tendril of energy reaching out from your energy center and connecting you to the tool. Visualize the energy suffusing the tool. Say,

> *(Name of tool), I welcome you.*
> *It is done.*

Cleansing Your Garden Space

Beginning a garden, or reworking a garden to be a spiritual workspace, necessitates cleaning. The area should be tidied up, extraneous or unsupportive objects removed, and in general the space should be prepared as if it were to be dedicated as sacred space…which is, in essence, what it is. Cleaning is the physical part; the spiritual aspect comes next. Cleansing involves removing negative or unsupportive energy from a space intended to be dedicated to a specific purpose.

INDOORS

Physical cleaning, as always, is the basis for spiritual cleansing. This is especially important if you're setting up living things in that space, such as plants. Clutter and buildup of dust and dirt can trap energy or slow down the healthy circulation of energy in your home. The first rule of beginning any magical work in any area of your home is to clean the area. You can dust, sweep, vacuum, and mop normally, but you can also add some magical support to those activities. Herbs are especially appropriate when preparing a space for gardening work.

OUTDOORS

Start by physically decluttering the area you intend to use for your outdoor garden space. If you have an existing garden space, clear out what you don't want to keep. Wash down any physical elements such as fences, walls, garden borders, raised beds, trellises, and so forth. Repair anything that is worn or broken. By physically clearing and cleaning, you're starting with a clean slate of a space. Returning the energy of the space to a neutral state is equally important. I like to do this by smoke cleansing, crumbling a blend of purifying herbs over smoldering incense charcoal set in a heatproof bowl filled with sand. My favorite for a cleansing like this is a mix of dried rosemary, dried sage, dried mugwort, and dried cedar. It's a solid, basic blend that disperses negative energy and leaves a fresh, quiet energy ready to be empowered with your intention for the space.

Strewing Herbs

Traditionally, herbs were scattered on floors to help freshen areas or deter pests. This version of strewing herbs helps break up negative energy. Sprinkle this mixture around the area you're going to be cleaning a while before you begin to get a head start on cleansing the energy of the space, and sweep it up as part of your physical cleaning routine. Alternatively, clean your space physically, then sprinkle the mixture to help freshen the energy if you feel more comfortable separating the two activities.

The amounts will depend on how big a space you're cleaning. The proportions given here will give you about ½ cup of mixture to scatter on the floor of the area you are preparing.

You'll Need: Bowl • 2 tablespoons fresh or dried rosemary • 2 tablespoons salt • 1 tablespoon pepper (powdered or cracked peppercorns) • 1 teaspoon cinnamon (powdered, or a stick roughly ground in a mortar and pestle) • Optional: Cedar, juniper, or pine needles (fresh or dried)

1   In the bowl, mix the ingredients together with your fingers.

2   Scoop up some mixture and scatter it over the floor in the desired area. As you do, visualize the purifying and cleansing attributes of the herbs filling the space.

3   Leave the herbs overnight if possible. If you have pets or cannot leave them, sweep them up when you have to.

You can use this mixture, add or subtract herbs, or come up with your own blend according to your needs and available supplies.

Waft the smoke rising from the incense blend around the garden area. If you can, walk around the perimeter spreading the smoke out and through the space with your hand, a bundle of fresh herbs, a fan, or feathers. Get right down so that the smoke can touch the soil itself. As you do this, visualize the smoke dissolving negativity; dispelling old, tired energy; and the soil sparkling with rejuvenation and fresh, fertile energy.

If smoke cleansing doesn't appeal to you, steep sprigs of your chosen herbs in fresh water to imbue it with their energies. First fill a clean jar with water, then add the sprigs of herbs. Place the jar in a sunny spot for 1–3 hours. This allows the solar energy to charge the water as well. You can pour the charged water into a spray bottle and disperse it that way, or use the sprigs of herbs to shake droplets around your garden space, dipping them into the water as required.

As community gardens are on public land, you probably won't have the kind of privacy you'd have at home. If necessary, adjust any of these rituals to be done wordlessly, tone down gestures if you feel uncomfortable or exposed, and bring premixed, blessed, or charged elements.

Another thing you can do at this point of the process is to use a stick or your finger to draw symbols in the soil for protection, abundance, and fertility. Choose a symbol that is personally meaningful to you, and draw it with intention. For an even more grounded, involved method, walk in the space in the shape of the symbol you're using, allowing your intention to flow into the ground with every footstep.

Bless Your Garden

Once something is cleansed, it is neutral space waiting for direction. Bless it to code it with your intention. Blessing gives your garden the best possible start. It calls in positive energy and specific intentions.

This elemental blessing can be used indoors or out, with a bit of adjusting on your part. As always, use this as a template for your own blessing if you feel drawn in a different direction. Prepare representations of the four elements before you begin. Arrange them however you like in the garden space.

Create sacred space in your preferred manner. It can be as simple as saying, "I recognize the innate spirituality of this land, and honor it. While I work here, may it be kept safe and free of negative energy." When you are ready, center and ground. Connect your personal energy to that of the garden area. Call upon the blessings of the four elements:

May this air always bring gentle breezes, to cool you when the heat is high, and carry the winged pollinators to enhance your fertility. May it bestir the oxygen you give us in return for the carbon dioxide you take in.

May this fire warm you and feed you as the sun above does in its daily pass. May the seeds respond to the light, the flowers open to it, and photosynthesis be fruitful and productive.

May this water nourish the seeds and roots to keep these plants growing strong. May the rains fall gently, and the ground be at the correct water levels for healthy growth.

May this earth grant you stability and abundance, the optimal levels of nutrients and minerals. We honor these organic beings who have gone before, whose bodies now nourish the soil.

I invoke Spirit, in the form of the pollinators. We honor the pollinators, whose actions ensure a multifaceted and healthy ecosystem. May the pollinators know that they are always welcome, and that their purpose is honored here.

May these all bless this garden, keep it well and safe. May it serve to be a refuge and a comfort.

Choose Your Planting Cycle and Design

A planting cycle is essentially figuring out when you can start planting in your hardiness zone. This knowledge, combined with your plan for what plants you intend to grow, will help you plan out scheduling for starting seedlings, sowing, and deciding what gets planted first. With this information, you can proceed with your layout plans. Are you going to reuse space later in the season after the first crop of early-bearing plants is done? Will you keep annual plants in place after they have finished blooming, or remove them to free up the location for something else?

Think about the cycles of the plants you've chosen—when they bloom, when they fruit, or when they bear their final product. Will you mix these up? Plant in groups according to when they go through part of the cycle at approximately the same time? Gathering this information will help you lock in your design for your garden layout.

DESIGN

This is where you get to brainstorm! No matter where your garden is, you can draw on color correspondences, symbology, and any other kinds of design elements you like. Sacred geometry for planning out placement? Numerology? Chase down any sort of information you like to help you decide how to arrange your garden space.

Beyond laying out your plants there are a few other things to keep in mind. Are your plants in containers of some kind? Choose the pots or containers according to magical goals. Buy clay and slab-built trays or decorative pots that you can line with waterproof material before setting a potted plant in them. (Be aware that unless clay is glazed and fired, it is not waterproof!) Or find a potter studio, community center, or makerspace and learn how to throw a pot on a wheel (very rewarding, and also very humbling).

Makerspaces can also offer woodworking sessions, which can allow you to build a set of basic shelves or a simple plant stand, or help you plan out how to build a raised garden bed or a trellis. A makerspace is a collaborative, supportive workspace where skills and equipment can be shared. They can support crafting, art, computer-related skills, electronics, and projects of all kinds. Look for a makerspace near you at https://makerspaces.make.co.

Create Your Garden Journal

Oh yes; the best part of gardening! (Other than being in touch with the earth and plants themselves, of course.) Over time, your garden journal will become an heirloom, a record of your journey within the plant kingdom, the energy you cultivated, and the land you tended. Your musings, your ideas, your experiments, and your plans make your garden journal a magical record, one that you can revisit or share with others.

A garden journal is an essential tool for any gardener, and doubly so for a green witch. Being able to keep notes on growth, yields, weather, and behavior of plants from year to year is essential in maintaining a grounded and informed garden.

Creating a record of your work helps you trace evolutions, challenges, how the garden responded to large weather events, and so forth. It collects your information on experiments with adding certain fertilizers at certain points, or choosing to prune or feed at different times in the moon phase cycle. Use your journal to make notes on everything from birds checking out your sacred space to how you dealt with aphids. If you have lived in the same place for many years, a garden journal enables you to trace how your interests evolve, and how your garden develops. It's always interesting to look back and see how much smaller a vine was, or how your vegetable focus shifted from harvest intended to be eaten fresh to a harvest intended for preserving.

The first step is to decide on the format for your garden record. There are two basic ways to physically collect your research and observations: in a binder or in a notebook.

As much as I love hardbound notebooks, my preference for a garden record is a binder. A binder allows you to add materials like plant tags and information sheets handed out with the plants you buy. A notebook can quickly grow unwieldy with these kinds of items inserted. Page protectors allow you to store envelopes with seeds in them (purchased or harvested from your plants, clearly labeled). You can also use page protectors to store pressed samples of leaves, flowers, small branches, or stems, glued to cardstock and inserted in the protector. Alternatively, you can laminate them on a piece of paper, punch holes in the paper, and add it to the binder directly.

> At the bare minimum, keep a garden journal in a tracker-style notebook. Write down when you plant things, when you see shoots, when things droop or look unhappy. Note down the days you watered or trimmed back, fertilized, or used compost tea. Keeping track will help you take the best care of your plants that you can.

Take photos of your garden frequently and print them out so you can paste them into the journal or create a parallel album for photos. Not only is this comforting to look at; it's a valuable reference for tracking growing seasons. Add photos of your garden at different times; this helps you track growth and development through the annual cycle. For indoor plants, this record allows you to trace a plant's development over the years, as well as seeing what its annual cycle is like, if it has one.

Your garden journal is the place to keep sketches of garden designs and layouts, actual and potential. It's also a place for a list of "someday" ideas. What would you like to do, but cannot at the moment because of budget, location, or other constraints? Those constraints can include "I have no idea how to do this right now" or "I can't think through all the steps to accomplish this"; this list is meant to be a hold-all for anything and everything.

GARDEN JOURNAL VERSUS YOUR GRIMOIRE

As a green witch, the lines between a garden journal and your grimoire or spiritual journal may blur significantly. Where you place and organize your information is up to you. You may want to keep your magical information separate from your garden information, or you may want to fold it all together. There's no right or wrong way to do it.

RECORDING SAMPLES AND HARVESTS

Taking samples is an important part of keeping a garden record. As a green witch, you probably take snips of your plants as they grow to use them in spellwork or herbal medicine. Here's how to proceed:

- With respect, extend your sense to the plant and inquire if you may take a sample or harvest a portion of it. If you get any feeling that is not a clear yes, don't touch it. Give water to the plant as an offering, whether it acquiesces or not.
- Don't uproot the entire plant. Carefully snip off a branch or a leaf, cutting at a 45-degree angle about a quarter inch above a leaf node to encourage more growth.
- Keep the samples damp to keep them as fresh as possible until you can press them. To keep cuttings fresh, fold them into a lightly dampened light cloth or paper towel, and slip it into a plastic bag. Don't forget to write down the date it was harvested.

As an alternative to physically harvesting a sample of the plant, you can photograph it, print it out (if you have a physical grimoire or garden journal, or use the digital photo if you keep a digital one), label it, and add it to the page recording the plant's information.

PRESSING A SAMPLE

If you do take a sample of the plant, you may want to press it to preserve it in your journal. The following project will describe the process for you. An easy way to press plants is with newspaper. This can be hard to find these days, so you can use flyers or other kinds of paper as well; just have a clean piece of paper in direct contact with the plant, such as blotting paper. (You can buy blotting paper at an art or craft store.) For the cardboard, you can deconstruct a shipping box and cut pieces from it.

PROJECT

Pressing Samples

Pressing a sample helps preserve it to keep as part of your garden's record.

You'll Need: Newspaper or blotting paper • Pieces of corrugated cardboard, roughly 8" × 10" • Large, heavy book • Cardstock (8" × 10") • Glue • Cotton swab or small paintbrush • Waxed paper • Small blank label • Pen

1 Lay the sample out as flat as possible on one layer of newspaper (with a few sheets in the layer). Fold one side over the sample or lay another few pieces of paper on top. Lay a piece of cardboard on top. Try to use corrugated board, which allows air to circulate better than a solid piece.

2 Begin the next layer of newspaper and samples, alternating with pieces of cardboard. (Think of it as a layer cake or a lasagna!)

3 When you have folded all the samples into paper, lay a heavy book or two on top and make sure the stack is out of the way. Leave it to dry.

4 Check every couple of days to see how the drying process is going. If the newspaper starts to get damp, trade it for fresh paper. Drying can take a week for thinner, lighter plant matter, or longer if you're pressing something with a fleshy stalk or thick leaves. The faster it dries, the better the color and overall condition will be.

5 Once the sample is dry, mount it by gluing it to a piece of cardstock. Use a cotton swab or small paintbrush to paint the glue on in a very light layer to avoid blobs of glue. Put a piece of waxed paper over the sample and put a heavy book on top of it to help the glued sample dry flat. Remove when dry.

6 On a label, identify the plant by its botanical name, common name(s), the location in which you found it, the date it was collected, and any other pertinent information you feel should be included. Glue the label to the corner of the card.

7 Insert the card into your garden journal.

Creating Records for Herbal Entries

One of the central parts of your garden journal will likely be the information you collect about plants, trees, and flowers. How you set up this information will be important to your work as a green witch. Recording information should be done clearly, concisely, and with attribution to the source and/or reference. There's a lot of information to include too; just noting down magical correspondences is limiting the ways in which you can draw on a plant's energy. Let's look at the different sections of an entry.

> This order and information is applicable to trees, flowers, and herbs; we'll use the word *plant* to stand in for all of these here.

1. **The name of the plant.** This is important in a variety of ways. First, include the botanical name, which never changes the way folk names can. Record common names too (and yes, there are usually more than one), including outdated ones. There is more than one plant known as mandrake, for example.

2. **Physical description and traits.** Describe how the plant looks. You can use a photo, a botanical illustration, or a sample of the actual plant as your source. Include information such as the shape of the leaf, stem, flowers, and/or fruit.

3. **Illustration.** You can draw this yourself, trace a botanical illustration, or photocopy a photo from a book. If you use someone else's work as an inspiration or a mechanical copy, note down the source.

4. **Toxicity/warnings.** Note any toxic warnings associated with the plant. This includes touching the leaves, juice, or sap, breathing in the scent, breathing in the smoke if burned, and ingesting it. Even if you don't plan to do these things, note them down anyway. This is critical information to include; make sure you write down the specifics.

5. **Geographic information.** This has more pertinence to growing plants indoors than outdoors, if you are growing something non-native or not suited to your hardiness zone, for example. What region

of the world does the plant grow in? What kinds of environments? If you know the planting zone for it, include that information. Also note down the region or locale to which the plant is native. (This information becomes important when you focus on working with local and native plants, an important part of green witchcraft.)

6. **Medical information.** Even if you don't intend to use the plant medicinally, write down this information; the knowledge is useful for rounding out your records. Note down what specific parts are used in particular treatments. You can draw on this information magically too; energy is energy, after all.

7. **Practical and historical uses.** This information may overlap with medicinal applications; for example, using lavender in strewing herbs to deter fleas, or cedar to repel moths.

8. **Traditional magical information.** What have past witches used this plant for? What are the magical uses that have become common in practice? What parts of the plant are used for specific purposes? Remember to note your sources for each bit of information.

9. **Your personal magical information.** This is just as important as traditional uses for the plant in question. Your personal experiences and interactions with it hold more weight in your magic than those of a practitioner a century ago. Record here your energy-sensing exercises, and your experiences and interactions with the plant. Cross-reference this information with the results you record of your spells and magical workings involving the plant.

10. **Examples of the plant.** A pressed sample of the plant (leaves, flowers, or other) is good to include in your entry. Alternatively, a small glassine envelope of crumbled dried plant matter can be glued or taped in.

If this looks like a lot of information, you're right, it is. You want your garden journal to be as complete as possible. The more complete the information is, the more knowledge you can draw from it. Following is a sample layout of what a journal entry for a specific plant or herb might look like. Feel free to copy it and place it into your gardening journal.

PLANT ENTRY

Date:

Name of the plant:

_____

Physical description and traits:

_____

_____

_____

Toxicity/Warnings:

_____

_____

_____

Geographic information:

_____

_____

_____

Medical information:

_____

_____

_____

Practical and historical uses:

_____

_____

_____

Traditional magical information:

_____

_____

_____

Your personal magical information:

_____

_____

_____

illustration/photograph

examples of the plant

Planning for Next Year's Garden

Winter or the off-season is a great time to review your gardening notes for the year that has ended. What worked? What failed? What worked but could have gone better? Sketch out alternate garden plans, experimenting with different locations or different plants. Look at your list of "someday" plants or ideas. Is the coming year the time to try one?

One of the pleasures of gardening is reviewing seed and plant catalogs, planning out the garden for the next year. Will you try a new variant? Stick with what worked last year? The sky's the limit when it comes to brainstorming. Indulge in the research, reading reviews on how certain varieties have grown in your climate or geographic area to help you make your decisions.

Online communities can offer you input from people in your area; you might even be able to trade seeds or seedlings. Botanical gardens or societies sometimes organize such trades or offer information sessions. Do a little research and see what you can find.

Chapter 6

Choose
What
to Plant

Plant What You Like

Choosing what to plant is the most exciting part of planning your witch's garden, and possibly also the most difficult. First of all: You should plant what makes you happy. There is no point to planting something that is used in magical work if you don't like it. A personal connection with your materials is essential, and if you actively dislike a plant and don't want to use it—whether it's the plant's look, scent, or magical energy that you aren't a fan of—there is absolutely no point in having it take up space that could be better used for a plant that has more positive associations for you.

A personal connection with your materials is an important consideration when selecting plants to grow. What have you worked with magically in the past that resonated with you? Whether it be dried plant matter you bought in a shop or online, or something you used in essential oil form or as a tisane or other infusion, if you have experience with it and like it, it can have more impact in your magical work than something else.

Refer back to Chapter 2 to refresh your memory about your magical goals and the purpose(s) of your garden, and for tips regarding how your garden's geographic location will affect your choices.

Personal connection is also why we grow things ourselves if possible. The amount of personal energy infused in a plant that you have cared for as it grows and develops helps key it to your magical work later. It also reduces the need for cleansing your materials before you use them—the act of neutralizing or dispelling negative energy or unwanted energies that have attached themselves to the herb or other type of plant before it found its way to you.

What follows in this chapter is a selection of plants that can be used in witchcraft. The plants are divided into the categories of:

- Flowers
- Herbs
- Fruit
- Vegetables
- Trees
- Mushrooms and fungi
- Ground cover and grains

These lists are in no way complete; they are simply suggestions with magical applications or symbolic energies listed.

Flowers

Most plants flower in some way; it's part of the natural cycle. Even plants you might not expect to flower do, albeit briefly or at long intervals, like cacti or succulents. When we think of flowers, however, we often mean a plant that is grown specifically for its blossoms. The flower of a plant carries a tidy bundle of energy, for it is the sexual organ of the plant, part of how the plant reproduces.

COLOR MEANINGS

Color carries its own energy, and so the color of a flower can subtly modify the plant's energies. Over time, different colors have been associated with different magical goals, and a list is included here for reference. However, as stated earlier in the chapter, your own personal associations with the plant, including its color, will influence your work with them. If you hate orange, there's no point in using it as one of your magical correspondences, no matter how many lists try to convince you that orange is associated with success.

Here's a basic list of color correspondences that I use:

- Red: life, passion, action, energy
- Pink: affection, friendship
- Orange: success, speed, career, action
- Yellow: intellectual matters, communication
- Light green: healing, wishes
- Dark green: prosperity, money, nature
- Light blue: truth, spirituality, tranquility, peace
- Dark blue: healing, justice
- Violet: mysticism, meditation, spirituality
- Purple: occult power, spirituality
- Black: protection, fertility, mystery
- Brown: stability, home, career
- White: purity, psychic development
- Grey: calm, spirit work, gentle closure, neutralizing energy or situations
- Silver: purity, divination, psychic work, feminine energy, spirit, lunar energy
- Gold: health, prosperity, solar energy, masculine energy

COMMON FLOWERS

Flowers can be grown for color, scent, and food, besides aesthetic pleasure. The energy they carry can be subtly different from the stalks or leaves; try working with each to see which energy you prefer. Flowers are part of the reproductive system of a plant, attracting pollinators who mix pollen from different plants as they travel. Once fertilized, seeds develop in the ovary portion of the flower. For this reason, flowers in general can be used for fertility or abundance magic. Here are some flowers commonly found in a green witch's garden.

Calendula

Calendula officinalis

Magically associated with protection, psychic abilities, dreams, success with legal issues, fidelity, healing, love, animals, and comfort.

How to Grow: Commonly known as pot marigolds, calendula is a hardy plant that can tolerate a wide range of light conditions, from lower light to full sun. They thrive in beds or containers but prefer cooler weather. The plants bloom throughout the growing season and will bloom more than once if you cut off older flowers. Provide regular water and a balanced fertilizer for best results.

Carnation

Dianthus spp.

Also known as gillyflower, the carnation has a wonderful healing energy and makes an excellent gift for the sick. Carnations are used magically for protection, strength, energy, luck, and healing.

How to Grow: Carnations are extremely rewarding plants to grow, in part because they tolerate a wide range of conditions. These free-flowering plants prefer soil that is slightly alkaline (like most plants) and will grow in containers or beds, forming low mounds that will bloom most heavily in the spring. Beware that Dianthus species may be toxic to pets, so if you're growing them inside keep the plant away from curious animals.

Chamomile

Chamaemelum nobile, Matricaria chamomilla

Two types of chamomile are popular: Roman chamomile and German chamomile. Chamomile is a soothing, calming herb, both when taken as an infused tea and when worked with magically. Chamomile is magically associated with money, love, sleep, meditation, purification, protection, and tranquility.

How to Grow: Members of the daisy family, these pretty and small flowers add a wildflower look wherever they are planted. They prefer to grow in full sun in well-drained (not soggy) beds or containers. The feeding requirements are light, but the plant will perform best if you apply fertilizer at planting time. Chamomile flowers appear in large numbers in the early midsummer and will continuously bloom until fall.

Daffodil

Narcissus spp.

Also known as narcissus and jonquil, the daffodil is an excellent flower to use in charms for love and charms for fertility. Magically, the daffodil is associated with luck, fertility, and love.

How to Grow: Daffodils thrive throughout most of the United States. These bulbs should be planted in the fall, before frost and snow. In the spring, the young daffodils will send up blooms, one of the early signs of a new growing season. Daffodils do best with bright or full sun to encourage blooming. Avoid planting them in soggy, low-lying areas where the bulbs may rot. Plant your bulbs with the pointed end facing up, about 3–6 inches apart.

Daisy

Leucanthemum vulgare,
Chrysanthemum leucanthemum

Also known as field daisy and ox-eye daisy, the daisy is commonly associated with love and flirtation. We have all plucked the petals from a daisy—"he loves me, he loves me not." Magically, the daisy is associated with love, hope, and innocence. Use the daisy in magic associated with children as well.

How to Grow: Sometimes listed by the name *C. leucanthemum*, the ox-eye daisy is the ideal wildflower. These yellow and white flowering perennials like to grow in full sun, or in slight shade to protect from midday sun, in beds of well-drained soil. Daisies cannot tolerate standing water, so make sure your growing area has plenty of drainage. Deadhead the flowers to encourage more blooms, and replace the plants every two or three years to keep them vibrant.

Gardenia

Gardenia spp.

Gardenia is an excellent flower that attracts tranquil energy to a place or individual. Adding gardenia petals to a healing sachet or using them in a healing ritual incorporates this tranquil energy and helps the healing move at a controlled pace. Gardenia is also commonly used in love spells and charms. Magically, gardenia is associated with harmony, healing, love, and peace.

How to Grow: Gardenias are known for their creamy white flowers and evocative early evening scent. These subtropical or tropical shrubs are commonly grown in containers in cooler regions, or can be used as landscape plants in warmer climates. Gardenias prefer rich, organic soil that is slightly acidic, so for best results use a specially formulated fertilizer for acid-loving plants. They do well in partly shaded conditions, but they are susceptible to sooty mold and fungus, so avoid drenching the foliage and letting it remain wet.

Geranium

Pelargonium spp.

Grown indoors or out, geraniums carry strong protective energy and extend this energy through the area around them. Red geraniums have traditionally been associated with protection. Rose geranium is used in love spells. Magically, geraniums are associated with fertility, love, healing, courage, and protection.

How to Grow: Native to South Africa, these plants are perennials that are typically used as annuals in cooler climates throughout North America. They excel as bedding plants, in container gardens, or in hanging baskets, where they flower freely throughout the growing season (encourage more blooms by snipping off dead flowers). Geraniums like slightly acidic soil and thrive in a rich, organic planting medium with plenty of regular water. Be aware that geraniums are toxic to both humans and animals.

Hyacinth

Muscari racemosum,
Hyacinthus non-scriptus

Both grape and wild hyacinths have a lovely spring-like scent. The perennial wild hyacinth, also known as the bluebell, is smaller and daintier than the cultivated grape hyacinth. Hyacinths bloom for only a short period of time, but in that short period produce a vibrant energy. Hyacinths are named for the youth of Greek legend, beloved of Apollo, whose accidental death Apollo commemorated by creating the flower. Hyacinths are magically associated with love, happiness, and protection.

How to Grow: Hyacinths are the harbingers of spring. These bulbs are frequently the first to pop through the soil in early spring, signaling the start of a new growing season. After the blooms begin to fade, snip them off. This will prevent seed formation and preserve the bulb's strength for another growing season. If seedpods form, remove them. In general, hyacinths are done blooming within a few weeks of the spring growing season. An established bed of hyacinths will often require little or no care for years. Plant bulbs in the fall in a sunny spot.

Iris

Iris florentina

Also known as flags, irises are a lovely spring flower magically used for purification and blessing as well as wisdom. The three petals are said to symbolize faith, wisdom, and valor. The root is called orris root, and when ground up it produces a mildly sweet powder used as a scent fixative in potpourri. Orris powder is also used for peace, harmony, and love.

How to Grow: Iris is a historically important plant that has been in cultivation for centuries. These flowering plants grow from rhizomes, or underground stems, that are planted in a sunny location in sandy, very well-drained soil. They are heavy feeders that require a good dose of fertilizer in the early spring to perform best. Every few years, dig up and divide the rhizomes to give new plants more room and increase your stock.

Jasmine

Jasminium spp.

Also known as jessamine, jasmine possesses a heady but delicate scent that is usually stronger at night. Because of this, it is often associated with the moon and feminine energy. Jasmine, which has long been associated with seduction and sensuality, is a perfumer's prized ingredient. Magically, jasmine is associated with love, meditation, spirituality, harmony, and prosperity.

How to Grow: There are multiple kinds of jasmine, and the most popular varieties reward their gardeners with a beautiful scent that comes in flushes. Jasmine is available as a vine or a shrub or even a small tree. They can be grown indoors in containers or outside on trellises or as border plants. Jasmine should be grown in full or partial sun, in a warm location with well-drained soil. Mature jasmine should be pruned to keep its shape.

Lavender

Lavandula spp.

Another perennial favorite, lavender is used frequently in magical and non-magical applications. Thanks to its gentle scent, it is an ideal herb to use in conjunction with magic for children, for it encourages relaxation and sleep. Magically, lavender is associated with peace, harmony, tranquility, love, purification, and healing.

How to Grow: With its soft leaves and purple flowers, lavender is a beloved member of the mint family. Suitable for containers or massed beds, lavender prefers full sun and well-drained, even slightly drier soil. The plants bloom in midsummer with masses of small purple flowers on graceful, small stalks. They are toxic to animals. To encourage long-term blooms, trim your lavender back by about one-third when it's done blooming.

Lilac

Syringa vulgaris

The sweet, wild scent of lilacs in late spring is a heady experience. The flowers of this shrub are usually white or shades of purple. Magically, they are used for protection and banishing negative energy.

How to Grow: The heavy scent of lilac is a sure indicator of summer throughout temperate North America. Grown as hedges or informal bushes, lilacs bloom with large clusters of flowers in a variety of colors. Some varieties of lilac can reach up to thirty feet at maturity, but dwarf varieties are generally under ten feet. Lilacs appreciate plenty of organic material in the soil and are considered low-maintenance shrubs. Prune your lilac for best results and to keep its shape.

Lily

Lilium spp.

The lily family is very large. In general, lilies are associated with protection and the elimination of hexes. Daylilies bring to mind the concept of cycles. In some cultures, lilies are associated with the concept of death and the afterlife, supporting the association with rebirth and cycles.

How to Grow: Lilies are grown from bulbs as perennial flowers that emerge from the ground in spring and bloom in the early summer or fall, depending on the type. Plant your new lily bulbs in the fall, before the ground freezes. If possible, plant the lilies about three times as deep as the height of the bulb, with the pointed side facing up, about 15–18 inches apart. Lilies prefer well-drained, rich soil in a location with lots of sun. When the new growth emerges, water them regularly and feed with a blooming fertilizer to encourage strong blooms. After the bloom is finished, cut off the flower stalk but do not remove old leaves until they are completely dead in the fall. These leaves help provide nourishment to the bulb to help prepare for next season.

Lily of the Valley

Convallaria magalis

This tiny cascade of white or cream-colored bell-shaped flowers has a delicate scent. Magically, it enhances concentration and mental ability and is used to encourage happiness.

How to Grow: Lily of the valley is a popular perennial ground cover in shady or semi-shady conditions, such as under trees. These spreading, low plants are tough and can easily take over a bed once they're established—consider using containers if space is an issue. Fertilize in the spring and provide regular watering for best results. Lily of the valley doesn't like to dry out too much. These plants are very toxic to people and animals alike.

Lupine

Lupinus spp.

With spikes upon which many small flowers grow, lupines come in many colors; blue lupines are called bluebonnets in the United States, so named for the shape of the flowers, which look like small bonnets. The seeds resemble small beans, which can be used for wish magic. Lupine can be used to enhance creativity and for magic associated with dogs.

How to Grow: Lupines are among the most popular perennials, beloved for their dramatic flower spikes. They do best planted in sandy, very well-drained soils with regular watering and cooler temperatures. Deadhead your lupines to encourage more blooms, and feed them regularly throughout the summer months. Start your lupine garden by spreading seeds in the spring or transplanting seedlings.

Pansy

Viola tricolor

Also known as heartsease, love-in-idleness, and Johnny-jump-up, the pansy is a hardy, cheerful-looking plant with multicolored flowers related to the violet. It blooms throughout the summer and comes in both annual and perennial varieties. Magically, it is used for divination, communication, happiness, and love.

How to Grow: Pansies are very popular and delicate flowering plants that are commonly used in container gardens and baskets, as well as massed beds. They like cooler temperatures and will suffer in hotter climates or heat spells. Plants bloom in the spring and early summer and are usually grown as annuals. They prefer very well-drained soils in full sun to partial shade and do best with lots of fertilizer.

Poppy

Papaver rhoeas

Also known as the corn poppy, the red poppy is a bright flower with a furry green stem and leaves. Although the red poppy is a gentle narcotic in large quantities, it is the white poppy that is toxic and the source of opium. Poppy seeds are used in cooking and baking, and sometimes oil is extracted to be used in cooking as well. Magically, the poppy is associated with tranquility, fertility, prosperity, love, sleep, and invisibility.

How to Grow: Red poppies are great for wildflower gardens. These annual flowers offer up delicate cup-shaped red blooms in the spring and summer. Poppies are commonly planted from seed but can also be found as small transplants. Poppies are known as low-maintenance plants that tolerate a wide range of light exposure and soil conditions. Remove older flowers to encourage better blooms. Red poppies are toxic to pets.

Primrose

Primula vulgaris

One of the first flowers to bloom in spring, the primrose is most commonly pale yellow, although white and pale pink species exist. They are a favorite of pollinators. Primroses are good for magic associated with children, protection, and new beginnings. They can be a nice addition to rites of passage. (Note: The common primrose bears no relation to the evening primrose.)

How to Grow: Primrose is an early spring bloomer that grows as a low ground cover in partly shaded areas. Primrose prefers cooler temperatures to germinate. The plants themselves are not demanding—they like average water and temperature and aren't picky about their preferred soil type. Use a standard fertilizer in the growing season to encourage best results.

Rose

Rosa spp.

Across cultures and throughout history, the rose is one of the most famous flowers. Folklore and literature have made the rose synonymous with love, although that is far from being the only association it carries. Roses create an atmosphere of beauty that encourages closeness with nature. The flower has a gentle scent, the intensity of which varies from genus to genus. Magically, the rose is associated with healing, divination, tranquility, harmony, psychic ability, spirituality, and protection.

How to Grow: Roses have a reputation as difficult plants, a reputation that has been cultivated by growers who are forever in pursuit of the perfect rose bloom. Many roses grow easily, however; check your local garden center for advice on which varieties will thrive in your environment. Roses grow as small, spiky shrubs in full sun. They like plenty of water in well-drained soil and should be regularly fed to encourage their blooms, which can appear in spring or summer. Rose bushes should be carefully pruned to encourage open growth and discourage sooty mold.

Snapdragon

Antirrhinum majus

Snapdragons have a lovely innocent energy. Magically, they are used for protection, particularly from illusion or deception, or to reflect negative energy to its source. Plant snapdragons along the perimeter of your garden to protect it.

How to Grow: Snapdragons are technically perennials that are typically treated as annuals in cooler-region gardens. They are also very popular container and window-box plants, with their characteristic long-lasting flowers. Mature plants can range in size from a few inches up to four feet tall. They like full sun but will grow in partial shade. Snapdragons like soil with plenty of organic material, regular watering, and an early-season dose of fertilizer. Flowers will appear throughout the growing season.

Sunflower

Helianthus spp.

Also known as Peruvian marigold, the sunflower is, of course, associated with the sun and its energy, which means it carries magical associations of happiness, success, and health. The sunflower is also associated with welcome and family. The plant's abundant seeds carry the magical associations of fertility. Sunflowers are excellent in a celebration ritual or during a summer solstice ritual. Germinate the seeds and then plant them to increase the energy of abundance in your garden in general. (Be sure you choose specific seeds meant for planting instead of planting random seeds, so you will know what size of sunflower to expect!)

How to Grow: Sunflowers have inspired writers and artists for centuries. These striking plants feature large flowers on tall stalks that may need to be staked up if the flower heads are too heavy. Sunflowers like plenty of light, moisture, and fertilizer—they don't like dry conditions and will turn brown in droughts. Perennial sunflowers spread by underground stems called rhizomes, so you can divide a patch every few years to increase your stock.

Tulip

Tulipa spp.

The chalice or cup-like shape of the tulip makes this flower ideal for use in prosperity and abundance magic. The tulip is also associated with protection, love, and happiness.

How to Grow: Tulips are a popular spring bulb that sends up delicate cupped flowers early in the growing season. Tulips have been extensively bred over the centuries to be available in a staggering array of colors. Tulips really shine when planted in massed beds, so their blooms will provide a bright splash of color in the garden while the other plants are still getting established. Tulip bulbs like rich soil and plenty of moisture. They do best in full sun.

Violet

Viola odorata

Also known as sweet violet, the violet is a delicate flower used for peace, hope, harmony, protection, luck, love, sleep, and tranquility. Use violet in charms and sachets designed to maintain tranquility and to encourage peace, particularly among people. Combine violet with lavender for a child's herbal pillow to aid sleep and calm nightmares. Violet also has aspects of fertility and abundance, which are reflected in how easily the plant propagates itself.

How to Grow: Violets are perennial plants that have been grown in Europe and Asia for hundreds of years. Commonly used as a ground cover, violets offer up small foliage and intensely fragrant flowers. They can thrive in light conditions ranging from full sun to partial shade, as long as they get enough moisture. Violets spread by underground roots but they aren't considered aggressive and are easy to control. Provide your violets regular water and fertilizer and look for flowers in the spring.

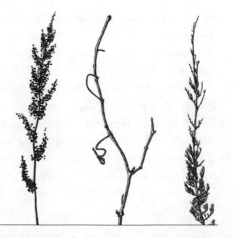

Herbs

Herbs are wonderfully flexible to use in all sorts of magical applications. Given restricted growing space, I'd turn to herbs as multi-use plants. They dry easily, pack a lot of energy in a small amount of foliage, have multiple magical correspondences associated with each herb, and can be used for regular cooking, magical cooking, and magical work. They are also aesthetically pleasing to look at, have pleasant scents, and are generally easy to care for. What's not to love?

This section is divided into culinary herbs (the kind you find in your pantry) and non-culinary herbs (the plants that are often used for magical purposes but aren't commonly used in the kitchen). Witchcraft makes use of all sorts of plants, many of which aren't classified as flowers, fruits, vegetables, shrubs, or another clear category. These non-culinary herbs have lots of uses.

A NOTE ON CINNAMON

It's actually possible to grow cinnamon in pots. Normally grown in subtropical to tropical climates, it can be grown indoors if your hardiness zone doesn't match the necessary requirements. Outdoors it can grow into a small tree, but potted and indoors (or grown in a container outside in summer and brought in for the winter) it can stay compact. The fresh leaves can be bruised and used in teas or for magic, or dried and used magically. To obtain something closer to the bark we're familiar with, cut small branches and dry them. They can be used in magic the way pantry cinnamon can. For scent, score the dried bark to release more of the aromatic oil.

COMMON CULINARY HERBS

Angelica

Angelica archangelica

Also known as archangel or angel's herb, this fragrant plant has been used throughout the centuries for improving digestion, flavoring wines and liqueurs, and making candy. Magically, it is particularly powerful when used for protection and purification.

How to Grow: Related to parsley, angelica is a less common herb but not especially difficult to grow as a short-lived perennial or biannual plant. Angelica blooms after two years of growth. Once done blooming, the plant will frequently die. Angelica likes somewhat cooler areas, so if you live in a hot area plant your angelica in a location that gets protection from the hottest sun. Always make sure your angelica gets plenty of water—it is sensitive to drought.

Basil

Ocimum basilicum

Also known as sweet basil and St. Joseph's wort, basil is commonly found in spice racks and in kitchen gardens all over Europe and the Americas. It is extremely versatile in the culinary arts and is an excellent all-purpose magical herb as well. Basil is used for prosperity, success, peace, protection, happiness, purification, tranquility, and love.

How to Grow: Basil is one of the most rewarding herbs to grow because it's so vigorous. Basil prefers warmth, plenty of water, and lots of rich, organic soil. It does equally well in the ground or in containers, and you can start to harvest your basil as soon as it's established (younger basil is less likely to be bitter). Basil prefers 6–8 hours of sunlight every day.

Bay

Laurus nobilis

Also known as sweet bay and sweet laurel, bay was used to crown the victor of games in ancient Greece and Rome. Bay is magically associated with success, wisdom, and divination. Write a wish on a bay leaf and burn it, or sleep with it under your pillow for dreams that offer some sort of guidance as to how to pursue your goal. (If you burn the bay leaf, make sure your area is well ventilated, for the smoke can be mildly hallucinogenic.)

How to Grow: In its native Mediterranean environment, bay is a hardy shrub or even a small tree whose leaves are harvested and dried. To grow your own, plant bay in a container or locate in a sunny section of the garden. Bay is only hardy in USDA hardiness zone 8 or higher, so in colder climates you'll have to move the bay plant inside during the colder months to protect it. Bay likes well-drained soil, but thanks to a shallow root system the plant is sensitive to drought and should be watered regularly.

Caraway

Carum carvi

The seed of the caraway plant is excellent to use for protection against negativity. It's also a good antitheft herb, so add some to the garden sachets you place outdoors to keep little animal intruders from nibbling at your plants, as well as in protective sachets or charms in your home. Magical associations include health, mental abilities, protection, fidelity, and antitheft.

How to Grow: Caraway is frequently grown from seed, with gardeners sowing seeds in shallow holes about a quarter inch deep in the early spring. Caraway likes plenty of light and organic, rich soil. Mature plants are about three feet tall and will bear seed the second year after planting. To harvest your caraway for seed, snip the plants when the fruit is ripe and then dry and separate the seeds from the pods. Caraway leaves are also edible.

COMMON CULINARY HERBS

Chives

Allium schoenoprasum

The smallest of the onion family, chives have a delicate oniony taste that isn't overwhelming. The flowers are also edible, and add a pretty pale lavender color when sprinkled on salads or egg dishes. Like onions, they excel at protection and absorbing negative energy.

How to Grow: Chives are easy to grow in either a container or in a garden bed, where they are often used as border plants. Chives will do well in full sun, but if you live in an area with intense midday sun, consider planting in a location with partial sunlight. Chives like regular water-ing and plenty of fertilizer to perform best. If you're planting outside, separate your chive clumps after a few years to increase your plant stock and encourage new shoots. Chive leaves can be harvested as soon as they are large enough to snip away.

Cinnamon

Cinnamomum spp.

Cinnamon is one of the must-have multipurpose herbs in a green witch's stock. It possesses a great amount of energy, and a pinch can be added to anything to rev up the power level. It is also excellent for spells and charms involving money. Magically, cinnamon is associated with success, action, healing, protection, energy, love, prosperity, and purification.

How to Grow: Cinnamon is harvested from the bark of cinnamon trees, which are native to the tropics. Unless you live in a tropical or subtropical climate, cinnamon should only be grown in containers indoors so you can provide the heat, humidity, and bright light that cinnamon prefers. Cinna-mon plants require regular water but aren't picky about fertilizer. Cinnamon bark is ready to harvest when plants reach three years of age, when it's possible to peel away the outer bark and get to the yellow interior bark that can then be dried and ground into the familiar cinnamon spice.

COMMON CULINARY HERBS

Dill

Anethum graveolens

Also known as dill weed, dill comes in two forms: seed and weed, which is the feathery dried leaves of the plant. Either may be used in green witch work. Dill is magically used for good fortune, tranquility, prosperity, lust, and protection.

How to Grow: Dill is a common and relatively easy herb to grow in most temperate climates. For best results, plant your dill seeds in a sunny location or locate your dill container in a spot with full sun. Provide steady water, but don't let your dill plant sit in water. Dill will set seeds in hot weather, so you can harvest the seeds as soon as the blooms have faded. To harvest dill, cut the entire plant at the stem and hang it upside down in a brown paper bag—the seeds will fall from the flowers on their own.

Mint

Mentha spp.

There is a wide variety of green or garden mints, which are versatile herbs to grow in a garden or on the kitchen windowsill. An infusion of the leaves will help ease most headaches, stimulate the appetite, and aid digestion. Magical associations are prosperity, joy, fertility, purification, love, and success.

How to Grow: Mint is one of the best herbs for beginning gardeners. Mint plants are vigorous perennials that grow in a wide variety of conditions. In fact, mint is so easy to grow it's known for taking over whole gardens. Mint loves plenty of moisture but doesn't like boggy or soggy ground and will thrive in all kinds of light conditions, from full sun to dappled shade. Keep your mint varieties well watered, and you'll be rewarded with a steady supply of leaves.

COMMON CULINARY HERBS

Nutmeg

Myristica fragrans

Medicinally, nutmeg quells nausea and soothes digestive problems (although it can be toxic in large doses). Magically, it is associated with psychic abilities, happiness, love, money, and health.

How to Grow: Nutmeg is harvested from trees that grow in tropical regions, making it a challenge for temperate gardeners to produce themselves. In their native environment, nutmeg trees can grow to almost one hundred feet and begin bearing fruit after about six years of growth. Nutmeg doesn't do well in containers, so you should only attempt to grow nutmeg if you live in a subtropical climate and have room for a full-sized tree.

Parsley

Petroselinum crispum

In ancient Greece, parsley was used for such varied purposes as sprinkling on corpses to neutralize the smell of decay and making victors' crowns to celebrate success. It is magically associated with power, strength, lust, purification, and prosperity. Both the seeds and the leaves can be used.

How to Grow: Parsley is a popular annual that is prized for its nutrient-packed leaves. Hardy throughout much of North America, parsley can be grown in garden plots outdoors or in containers on your windowsill. Parsley likes a bright spot with plenty of water, but the well-mannered plants are relatively slow-growing and won't spread far. Harvest parsley when the plant reaches about six inches in height, cutting stems as needed.

COMMON CULINARY HERBS

Rosemary

Rosmarinus officinalis

Practical applications of rosemary include use as a skin tonic applied externally and as a hair rinse to add shine to dark hair and soothe itchy scalp. An infusion taken as a tea will help ease a headache. Magical associations include protection, improving memory, wisdom, health, and healing.

How to Grow: Rosemary is a hardy evergreen shrub that is often grown as an ornamental plant as well as a culinary or magical herb. Rosemary does best in sunny locations that provide plenty of warmth. The plant is drought tolerant, so don't overwater your rosemary, and it responds well to pruning.

Sage

Salvia spp.

Sage is perhaps the herb most commonly used for purification and protection. An infusion taken as a tea will help settle a sour stomach and ease digestion and can help calm anxiety as well. Magical associations include purification and protection, wisdom, health, and long life.

How to Grow: Sage is a common herb with slightly fuzzy leaves that thrives in containers as well as in regular garden beds. Sage plants like full sun, but if you live in a warmer climate with strong sun, consider providing later-afternoon shade to protect your plant from the harshest sun. Sage plants should be allowed to grow unchecked for a season before you start harvesting leaves. Once the plant is mature, you can harvest leaves as needed. Sage likes drier conditions; the plant should never be allowed to sit in water.

COMMON CULINARY HERBS

Tarragon

Artemisia dracunculus

This herb can be used to enhance confidence, strength, and protection. It can also be used to remove negative energy, and to promote emotional healing. Medicinally, tarragon tea can be used to promote recovery from illness and settle digestive issues.

How to Grow: Tarragon is a vigorous herb that does well in sunny areas. The plant tends to develop vigorous roots, so it's somewhat more drought tolerant than many herbs and can even grow in sandy soil. Adding a layer of mulch or other soil cover will make your tarragon even more hardy. Harvest leaves as soon as the plant is established.

Thyme

Thymus vulgaris

Used magically for protection and courage, thyme also can be used medicinally for sore throats. The oil has antiseptic and fungicidal properties, and can repel pests; add a few drops to a cup of water and spray it to help keep creepy-crawlies away. Magically, it can also help ease grief, uplift your mood, and clear negative energy.

How to Grow: Thyme is one of the easier herbs to grow. It thrives in full sunlight in a well-drained container or garden patch. Thyme has a well-deserved reputation as being somewhat drought tolerant, so err on the side of less water, as it will fail if it's allowed to sit in water. Thyme isn't picky about fertilizer, so use a controlled-release fertilizer, and it likes heat. Thyme is a perennial, so harvesting will encourage the plant to become fuller and more vigorous.

COMMON CULINARY HERBS	NON-CULINARY HERBS

Verbena

Verbena officinalis, Verbena spp.

Also known as vervain, enchanter's herb, herb of grace, and van van, verbena is an excellent all-purpose herb. Medicinally, an infusion of verbena helps calm headaches, eases stress, and makes a relaxing bedtime tea. Magically versatile, verbena is associated with divination, protection, inspiration, love, peace, tranquility, healing, prosperity, skill in artistic performance, and the reversal of negative activity. Make a verbena oil by infusing the fresh plant in a light olive oil or grapeseed oil to use as a standard blessing/protection oil. Add crumbled verbena leaves to any sachet to round out its positive energies. It is an excellent all-purpose herb to add to any charm bag or spell to encourage success.

How to Grow: Verbena is a perennial herb that is frequently grown as an annual in warmer regions. It also thrives in containers. Verbena likes full sun and well-drained soils—it's sensitive to being overwatered and should dry out between waterings. Regular fertilizer will help the plant achieve its mature size faster.

Comfrey

Symphytum officinale

Also known as boneset or knitbone, comfrey is renowned as a healing herb. Magically, it is associated with health, healing, protection during travel, and prosperity.

How to Grow: Comfrey is a highly adaptable perennial that grows quickly under the right conditions. The plant likes at least a few hours of full sunlight every day and isn't picky about the soil conditions as long as there is good drainage and regular water. Mature comfrey grows from a strong root system; plants will die back in the fall and emerge again from roots every spring. Comfrey spreads easily from wild-sown seed, so established plots may need control to prevent aggressive spreading.

NON-CULINARY HERBS

Foxglove

Digitalis purpurea

Foxglove flowers are shaped like fingers of a glove; in fact, the Latin name comes from the word for *finger*. Used medically as a cardiac stimulant, foxglove is toxic unless administered in precisely calculated doses, and should not be used at home in any way that involves consuming or applying the plant matter to skin, nor should you drink infusions or breathe the smoke of the burning leaves. Magically, it is said to carry energy that pleases fairy folk, so plant it or carry it to enhance your communication with them. It can be used for banishing.

How to Grow: Foxglove plants are prized for their bell-shaped, drooping flowers that rise on tall stalks. Typically grown as biennials that last only for two years, foxglove is a common garden plant throughout the temperate United States. Foxglove can grow in a range of light and soil conditions, with mature plants reaching six feet in height. Provide younger plants with plenty of consistent watering and increase water on hot days, as the plant will wilt in extreme heat.

Lady's Mantle

Alchemilla vulgaris

Used medicinally as an astringent and an anti-inflammatory, this plant is named for the scalloped leaf shape that is said to be reminiscent of the edges of a cloak; the lady referred to is the Virgin Mary. Magically, it is used to promote calm sleep and healing from the past, and can add extra energy to any magic being done for or by women.

How to Grow: Lady's mantle is prized for both its beautiful foliage and its long-lasting yellow flowers. The perennial plant grows easily from seeds sown directly in the garden, transplants, or cuttings, reaching a mature size of about two feet tall. Lady's mantle prefers bright locations and regular watering, although older plants are more drought tolerant. In hotter climates, provide afternoon protection from direct sunlight.

Mugwort

Artemisia vulgaris

Also known as artemisia and sailor's tobacco, mugwort is another ubiquitous witchy herb. A decoction of the leaves is said to help open your mind before you try divination. Magically, it is associated with prophetic dreams and divination, relaxation and tranquility, protection, banishing, and consecration.

How to Grow: Mugwort is a hardy perennial that is popular with pollinators and prized for its distinctive smell. It is a vigorous plant that can reach up to six feet in height, with dark green stems that can look slightly purple as if stained with wine. Mugwort likes full sun but can tolerate somewhat shadier conditions. Once established, mugwort can be aggressive, spreading from underground roots, so planting in containers is a good way to control it in the garden.

Mullein

Verbascum thapsus

Medicinally, mullein is used to soothe coughs, among many other uses; it is classified as an emollient, demulcent, and astringent herb. The hair–like fuzz on the leaves can be irritating to the mouth and throat, so make sure to strain it if you make a tea. Magically, mullein protects against danger and drives away negative energy. The plant has a thick mucilaginous sap, and when dry this contributes to its flammability. Mullein was used as tinder, and the flower spikes can be made into candle–like torches.

How to Grow: Mullein is a plant that commonly grows in roadside ditches or patches but does double duty as a land-scape or garden plant. With a flower stalk that can reach up to six feet bearing yellow flowers on tall cones, mullein is a striking specimen plant that tolerates full sun and dry soil. It's also popular with pol-linators and will bring birds and bees into your growing space.

NON-CULINARY HERBS

Valerian

Valeriana officinalis

Medicinally, valerian has sedative properties, and can also help relieve pain. Magically, it helps with self-confidence, finding the positive in a negative situation, and turning a negative situation to your benefit.

How to Grow: Valerian is a perennial herb that grows readily and easily in a wide range of conditions and spreads easily through wild-sown seeds. Mature valerian thrives in sunny conditions, growing into mature plants up to five feet tall and bearing white flowers. This plant is known for its cold tolerance and will emerge from the ground every spring even in cold regions. During the growing season, valerian prefers regular moisture. Mulching around the base of the plant will help conserve water in the soil and protect the plant.

Vervain

Verbena officinalis

Also an all-purpose culinary herb more often called verbena in that context, vervain is sometimes called the enchanter's herb for its wide and varied magical applications. It can be used to cleanse, purify, and protect. It is also a popular herb for enhancing psychic abilities and divinatory work. A pinch of vervain added to any charm or spell can increase the spell's chances of success. Medicinally, vervain can be used to reduce stress.

How to Grow: In its native range, vervain grows commonly along roadsides in Europe, where it thrives in full sun without supplemental moisture. In the garden, vervain blooms even during the hottest parts of the summer when there is little rain. The plant can grow in a large range of soil conditions, but doesn't like wet or soggy feet. Removing older flowers will encourage the plant to continue its bloom throughout the season.

NON-CULINARY HERBS

Wormwood

Artemisia absinthium

Wormwood can be used to keep away pests, and was a common addition to strewing herbs for this reason. Medicinally, wormwood is used as a tonic and stimulant. Extract of wormwood is used to make the liquor known as absinthe. Magical uses for wormwood include uncrossing or breaking a streak of bad luck, exorcism, banishing negative energy, enhancing psychic powers, and protection during travel.

How to Grow: Wormwood features beautiful silvery foliage and small yellow flowers on low, spreading plants that rarely get more than three feet tall. It prefers full sun but can tolerate some shade, and has high tolerance for drought and substandard soils. It is not considered aggressive and should be replaced with new plants or divided at the beginning of every growing season.

Yarrow

Achillea millefolium

Also known as milfoil, millefeuille, yarroway, or bloodwort, yarrow is a common garden herb grown for its attractive silvery foliage. The leaves and stem of yarrow, harvested in late summer, have traditionally been used as a poultice to stanch bleeding. Magically, it is used for courage, healing, and love.

How to Grow: Depending on where you are, common yarrow is either a landscape plant with yellow flowers or a noxious weed that spreads without regard for other plants. A perennial, yarrow forms a small shrub about three feet tall and three feet wide. It does well in full sun and is tolerant of a wide range of soil conditions. Yarrow also can tolerate colder climates and, once established, is highly drought tolerant.

Fruit

Fruit comes from trees, bushes, or canes. In this section we concentrate on the fruit itself. We will discuss some of these plants again in the Trees section later in this chapter; the tree and wood of the plant may have slightly different associations or applications.

Fruit is a plant's method of reproducing itself and carries an energy based in fertility and abundance. All fruit carries seeds, which are the beginning of life. Whether we consume the seeds or not, their fertile energy permeates the whole fruit. Fruit is also a great way to consume seasonal energy, for different fruits appear at different points of the seasonal cycle.

MAGICAL ASSOCIATIONS OF FRUIT

Here's a brief list of common fruits and their magical associations:

- Apple: health, longevity, love
- Banana: fertility, strength
- Blackberries: prosperity, protection, abundance
- Blueberries: tranquility, peace, protection, prosperity
- Cherry: divination, love
- Cranberries: protection, healing
- Grape: prosperity, fertility
- Lemon: purification, protection, health
- Lime: happiness, purification, healing
- Mango: spirituality, happiness
- Melons: love, peace
- Orange: joy, health, purification
- Peach: spirituality, fertility, love, harmony
- Pear: health, prosperity, love
- Pineapple: prosperity, luck, protection
- Plum: love, tranquility
- Raspberries: strength, courage, healing
- Strawberries: love, peace, happiness, luck

When it comes to growing fruit yourself, your options depend on what you want to grow and where you live. Bananas, for example, are a tropical herb that cannot tolerate frost and require huge amounts of water and fertilizer to thrive. By contrast, cranberries grow in vines that clamber along peat-based, acidic soil in bogs in the American northeast. Other tropical or subtropical fruits include mango, pineapple, and most citrus, while fruits like cherries and apples thrive in temperature regions with hard winters. No matter which fruit you're interested in growing, following two basic principles can help you have success:

> Cherry juice can be used as a substitute for blood in spells.

1. **Ensure this fruit grows well in your location.** Good sources of information include local garden centers, your county extension office, garden clubs, and other avid gardeners. Ultimately, your success will depend on growing the right fruit in the right place. If you're set on growing a fruit that doesn't thrive in your area, you can consider growing it inside, but be aware that most fruits are borne on trees and don't adjust easily to indoor cultivation.
2. **Follow planting, pruning, and feeding instructions for your chosen fruits.** A fruit tree is a long-term investment, with many hardwood fruit trees living and bearing fruit for decades. Before planting a fruit tree, ensure that you're planning for its mature size and that it will complement your growing space for years to come.

Vegetables

Like fruit, a vegetable is a visible seed container, and vegetables thus carry the magical associations of cycles and fertility. When you cook, therefore, you can also choose them for their magical associations.

Who can resist puns in their gardening? If you're looking for a sturdy tomato, the Mountain Magic hybrid has been bred to resist disease, while producing a sweet, small fruit. If you want to grow broccoli, the Green Magic hybrid is adaptable and matures in late summer to early fall, while Eastern Magic broccoli does well in the long days and high heat of the northeast of North America. Perhaps the White Magic cauliflower interests you, or the Magic Molly purple fingerling potato? Have fun with seed and starter catalogs!

MAGICAL ASSOCIATIONS OF VEGETABLES

Here's a brief list of common vegetables and their magical associations:

- Beans: love, family, protection
- Beets: fertility, grounding
- Broccoli: protection, abundance
- Cabbage: protection, prosperity
- Carrots: fertility, health
- Cauliflower: protection, fertility
- Celery: love, tranquility, concentration
- Corn: protection, divination, luck, Goddess offerings, protection of home, fertility spells, rituals for safe childbirth, infant protection
- Cucumber: fertility, healing, harmony
- Garlic: healing, protection, banishing, purification
- Leek: protection, harmony
- Lettuce: fertility, peace, harmony, protection
- Mushroom: strength, courage, healing, protection
- Olives: healing, peace, lust, protection, potency, fertility rituals
- Onion: protection, exorcism, healing, prosperity
- Peas: love, abundance
- Potatoes: fertility, protection, abundance
- Squash: abundance, harmony
- Tomato: protection, love

Vegetables can be used as vehicles for magic and spells, as well as for their inherent energies. For example, beet juice can be used as a substitute for blood in spells, while potatoes can be used as poppets, stand-ins for the target of healing or protection, for example.

Similar to growing fruits, which vegetables you grow is largely determined by where you live and what thrives in your area. The good news is that most of your favorite vegetables are much less of a commitment than a fruit tree, and most of them can be easily adapted to container culture. When you're planning a vegetable garden, a few pointers can help you get a better harvest, including:

- **Consider starting your vegetables from seed indoors before the growing season starts.** Growing from seed may require a few extra steps, including germinating and setting up a grow area inside with lights, but there are some powerful advantages, including access to dozens or even hundreds of varieties you can't find growing as transplants in your local garden center. Also, with some practice, you'll learn to produce much healthier seedlings than you can usually buy. Finally, you'll extend your growing season by several weeks by starting seedlings inside while it's still too cold to plant outside.

- **Prepare your garden plot or containers for your crop.** Most vegetables do better in rich, loamy soil with plenty of organic material. Prepare your garden plot by mixing in compost, peat, organic material, and, if you're using them, soil amendments like bone meal or blood meal. The same applies for containers, which allow you precise control over the growing environment.

- **Work ahead of time to build any structures you will need.** This includes fencing to keep out animals, trellises to support beans or cucumbers, or cages for indeterminate tomatoes.

- **Plan your irrigation.** Vegetables will need a steady supply of water to bear well. Before you actually plant, make

sure you'll be able to deliver adequate water, whether that means simply running a hose to your vegetable patch or installing some kind of automatic watering.

Growing great vegetables doesn't happen by accident. So whether you're planning a fully organic garden or a hydroponic indoor garden, researching and planning your garden before actually dropping seeds into soil will be time well spent.

Trees

While we tend to focus on herbs in witchcraft, we also work with wood, often when something more physically stable or permanent is required. The green witch's staff and stang, for example, are made of wood, as is the more traditional witch's tool, the wand. Sticks and twigs form the basis of many protective amulets, as do rounds cut from the cross-section of branches and inscribed with symbols.

> The parts of trees that can be used include bark, leaves, and inner wood.

MAGICAL ASSOCIATIONS OF TREES

Here are the magical associations of common trees:

- **Apple (*Pyrus malus*):** Apple trees are found all over the Northern Hemisphere. Their widespread availability and fertile abundance bring to mind their association with life, longevity, and fertility. Magically, apple trees are associated with love, healing, harmony, and longevity.
- **Ash (*Fraxinus excelsior*):** Ash is one of the trees considered by some European cultures to be the World Tree. Magically, ash is associated with water, strength, intellect, willpower, protection, justice, balance and harmony, skill, travel, weather, and wisdom.

- **Birch (*Betula* spp.):** The traditional witch's broom is made of birch twigs. Magically, birch is associated with cleansing, protection, and purification. It is also associated with children; cradles were often made of birch wood.

- **Cedar (*Thuja occidentalis*—yellow cedar; *Juniperus virginiana*—red cedar):** Another precious wood that is recognized by many cultures as magical and powerful, cedar has been known throughout the ages for its protective qualities as well as its ability to repel insects and pests. With its aromatic scent, cedar was often given as an offering. Magically, cedar is associated with healing, spirituality, purification, protection, prosperity, and harmony.

- **Elder (*Sambucus canadensis, Sambucus nigra*):** Elder is also known as witchwood. It is said that bad luck will fall upon anyone who does not ask the tree's permission three times before harvesting any part of it. Folklore associates the elder with the crone aspect of the Goddess and with witches, and thus elder wood is rarely used to make furniture or as firewood for fear of incurring their wrath. Medicinally, elder bark is used as a diuretic, purgative, and emetic. The berries are used as a laxative and diuretic and also induce perspiration, and the leaves are used as an external emollient for irritated skin, sprains, and bruises. An infusion of elderflowers taken as a tea stimulates perspiration, thus helping the body to work through a cold or illness, and also helps loosen chest and sinus congestion. Elderflower water makes an excellent topical application for irritated skin, including problems such as sunburn and acne, as well as an eyewash. Magically, elder wood is associated with protection (especially against being struck by lightning), prosperity, and healing.

- **Hawthorn (*Crataegus oxyacantha*):** Also known as may tree, mayflower, thorn, whitethorn, and haw, the hawthorn shrub was often used as a boundary marker. In fact, *haw* is an old word for "hedge." Hawthorn is a magical tree. If it grows together with an oak and ash tree, it is said that the fairy folk can be seen among the trees. Even where it grows alone, hawthorn is considered to be a fairy favorite. Like oak, the hawthorn produces hard wood and great heat when burned. Magical associations include fertility, harmony, happiness, the otherworld, and protection.

- **Hazel (*Corylus avellana*):** The hazel tree has long been associated in European folklore with wisdom. Gods and mythological figures associated with the hazel include Thor, Brigid, and Apollo. The nuts and branches are used for magic, and the hazel is associated with luck, fertility, protection, and wish granting.

- **Honeysuckle (*Lonicera caprifolium, Lonicera periclymenum*):** Also known as woodbine or hedge-tree, the honeysuckle is associated with liminal or transitional states. The scent of honeysuckle flowers is strongest in the evening. Magical associations include psychic awareness, harmony, healing, prosperity, and happiness.

- **Lilac (*Syringa* spp.):** Beautiful springtime flowers with a sweet, full scent can be used to make floral water and flavored sugar. Lilacs are associated with protection, beauty, love, psychic abilities, purification, and prosperity.

- **Maple (*Acer* spp.):** Maple is another popular tree used for cabinetry and by artisans. It is also a source of dye and maple sugar. Magically, maple is used for love, prosperity, life and health, and general abundance.

- **Oak (*Quercus robur*):** Oak is one of those traditional woods that are firmly entrenched in folklore and is magically associated with defense, thunder, strength, courage, healing, longevity, protection, and good fortune. Because the wood is very strong and durable and possesses a certain reputation for indestructibility, oak has been used in home construction and in shipbuilding. The bark is used to tan leather and as a dye. Acorns, the fruit of the oak tree, are symbols of fertility. When found growing in oak trees, mistletoe was considered to be particularly potent by the druids and was important in their magical work.

- **Pine (*Pinus* spp.):** Commonly used in building and construction, the pine is one of the most common trees in North

America. Its resin is used for the creation of turpentine and soaps, and for the production of rosin. Amber, one of the most beloved gems for magical jewelry, is fossilized pine sap. Pine oil, another product of the pine tree, is commonly added to household cleansing products, proof that the scent is associated with a sense of purification. Magically, pine is used for cleansing and purification, healing, clarity of mind, prosperity, and protection from evil.

- **Poplar (*Populus* spp.):** Also known as aspen, poplar's magical associations include prosperity, communication, exorcism, and purification.
- **Rowan (*Pyrus aucuparia, Sorbus aucuparia*):** Rowan is also known as quicken, hornbeam, witchwood, and mountain ash (although it is technically not a true ash, it is so called due to the similarity of the leaves). Rowan berries have been used in brewing, and the bark has been used for tanning and as a dye. Curiously, rowan has been said to be both a favorite of witches and fairies and anathema to them. Magical associations include improving psychic powers, divination, healing, protection from evil, peace, creativity, success, and change and transformation.
- **Willow (*Salix alba*):** The white willow, also known as the weeping willow, has long, flexible branches that have been used for centuries to be woven into what we know as wickerwork. Long associated with the moon, the willow has a great affinity for water and is often found growing near it. In folklore, the willow is associated with the Goddess and feminine cycles. Thanks to the ability of cuttings to easily and quickly recover from trauma, willow is also associated with growth and renewal. Magical associations of willow include love, tranquility, harmony, protection, and healing.
- **Witch hazel (*Hamamelis virginiana*):** Also known as snapping hazelnut, for the spontaneous cracking open of its seedpods, witch hazel has long been used as a poultice for bruises and swellings. Witch hazel extracts are used for their astringent properties. Magical associations include protection, healing, and peace.

- **Yew (*Taxus baccata*):** Yew is poisonous, which may be one of the reasons it is so closely associated with death. It is a European tree that figures largely in the lore of witchcraft and natural magic. The yew produces a very hard wood and was used where construction required an unyielding, inflexible structure. Magically, it is associated with spirits and the otherworld.

Mushrooms and Fungi

Mushrooms and fungi are often overlooked as part of a garden. You don't plant them the way you plant herbs or flowers, and they don't need the same kind of care. They're a fascinating thing to cultivate, however. Mushrooms are the most commonly recognized fungi. The cultivation of fungi is an interesting undertaking that offers you the chance to explore the energies connected to growing things that we don't often associate with a home garden.

Fungi are heavily associated with organic recycling, destruction, and reconstruction. They're a natural participant in the process of decomposition, the transformative process through which organic matter is broken down and returned to its base elements. In this way, they also represent a change or transformation from one state to another. Mushrooms and fungi are often associated with the underworld, partially because of their involvement in the process of breaking down organic matter after death, but also because in many cultural myths a deity or hero figure dies and descends to the underworld or afterlife to be symbolically deconstructed, then returns to the world with new insight. The association of psychedelic effects with some mushrooms is also transformative. Altering perception offers a different take on things, allowing you to change your point of view to gain insight. The symbolism and associated magical energy are valuable for a witch.

Fun fact: Yeast is a kind of fungus.

GROWING FUNGI

You can grow fungi any time; there's not a specific time of year they need to be started or harvested. Before you begin, establish your purpose for growing fungi: Will you be using them for food? Or ornamentally, with the intention to explore their energies in a non-ingested way?

Growing fungi generally requires a controlled environment. Cultivating a specific strain can be a challenge, because spores are everywhere, especially in soil and growing substrate. For this reason, special substrates can be purchased that have been sterilized to neutralize spores, meaning that only the ones you introduce will grow. Logs are a common place to grow fungi, both indoors and out.

> Unlike plants, mushrooms don't feed themselves via photosynthesis. They take all their nutrients from their growing medium, via the process of decomposition.

Instead of sourcing seeds, as you would with a plant, fungi require spores. These are often sold as plugs, which are wooden pegs that have been colonized with the fungi spores. These pegs are then hammered into a log. Other fungi require different substrate or growing material, such as sawdust or grains.

Mushrooms

Your supplier will have instructions on how to cultivate the fungus, with specifics regarding temperature and humidity. Starting out with a kit is a good idea if you're new to growing mushrooms. Growing indoors provides more easily controlled conditions, and mushroom cultivators sell kits that make it easy to grow exotic mushrooms.

MYCORRHIZAE

Mycorrhizae are microscopic fungi that colonize a plant's roots. They engage in a beneficial relationship with both the plants and the soil, increasing nutrient uptake for the roots of the plants while working to balance nutrients or rehabilitate poor soil. In this way, mycorrhizae support the plant in times of disease or poor growing conditions. While not a fungus you can grow, mycorrhizae are fascinating and can offer you more insight into the underworld aspect of witchcraft. In green witchcraft, the fallow or resting period is recognized as critical to balance the growth and expansion most people recognize as gardening and agriculture. Mycorrhizae are an important aspect of what happens underground, a link between the plant and the soil around it. It can even extend to a communication system connecting the plant to the other plants around it.

> If you're interested in growing mushrooms at home, check out "Spawning a Mycelial Mélange: How to Grow Mushrooms Outdoors" at the Gardner's Path website.

Ground Cover and Grains

What if you're not really interested in a formal garden, with the maintenance and in-depth hands-on interaction? If you have open spaces, or if you want low-maintenance plants while still interacting with the life cycle of flora, consider sowing cover-crop seeds or plants for ground cover in your available garden space. Cover crops are planted to nourish and protect the soil instead of for a specific harvest. If planted over winter, they can be plowed into the soil to feed it and restore nutrients lost to a previous crop, even before they reach maturity. If you choose to do this, look for local or native plants, both to work with flora that will grow easily in your location and to support local pollinators.

Another option to consider is grains. They protect the ground, provide space and support for local fauna, and yield a crop at the end of the growing season that can be used magically, even if you don't harvest a huge amount. Grains do require care at the end of the season, as they will need to be cut down, but the straw can be used for crafts, donated, or mulched.

Depending on your climate, there will be at least a few grains that you will be able to grow. Research them and see what kind of environment they require. Some grains can be sown in late fall to overwinter in the ground, while others grow better when planted in the spring. Again, your hardiness zone and the kind of grain you plant will help you choose which technique to try.

Harvesting may sound daunting, but you can walk through your patch of grain and cut off the heads with pruning shears, catching them in a bucket. Alternatively, cut off a foot or so of the stalk and bundle it together like a bouquet, tying it with string. Allow the heads to dry for a couple of weeks. The fun part of threshing comes next, laying them out on a tarp or old sheet and whacking them with a stick or bat, or stomping them with your feet, to loosen the grain. You can also use a pillowcase, tying the bottom shut with string and whacking it against a fence or a wall. Gather the loose grain from the straw, remove the chaff and dust by tossing the grain up into the air from a bowl and catching it again, allowing the wind to help carry away the dust. A fan can help if it's a still day or you're working inside.

Store your dried grains in firmly closed jars. If you're concerned that some moisture might remain, you can bake the grains lightly in a 135°F oven for 30 minutes, or use a dehydrator. You can grind your grain in a heavy blender or coffee mill to make flour.

You don't have to plant acres of grain. Something to remember about magic is that the important part of an ingredient or supply is the energy, not the amount. So go ahead and grow a grain, grind it, and add a pinch to whatever flour you're using for bread, oatcakes, or whatever you're making for an offering or magical meal.

OATS AND OATSTRAW (AVENA SATIVA)

Sativa means "cultivated," and oats are one of the oldest farmed crops. They do well in cool, wet environments, and are less likely than crops such as wheat or rye to fall prey to water-based diseases. You can sow oats in late fall for a summer harvest, or spring for a fall harvest. Oats go dormant in the heat of summer.

Harvest the oats when the seed heads begin to turn from green to gold, when the grain is still soft. They cure and finish ripening while resting after harvest. Oats need to have the hull removed in order to use the grain inside. You can do this by lightly pulsing the dried grain in a blender and then sifting through the cracked grain to remove the hull.

Hull-free oat strains are now available, greatly reducing the amount of work required to process them if you wish to take advantage of the grain oats produce.

Magically, oats represent prosperity and abundance. The oat plant carries energies of security, healing, relaxation, and grounding. In historical medical use, oats served antispasmodic and anti-inflammatory purposes. They were also used as a uterine tonic to help soothe what were once dismissively called "women's problems"; knowing that oats are full of vitamins and minerals, especially those that support the central nervous system, it makes sense that they would be used to treat issues related to the female reproductive system.

Oatstraw, the stem of the oat plant that remains after you thresh the grain, is surprisingly useful. You can make corn dollies with it (see Chapter 7 for information on this tradition), but there are also health benefits. If your system is stressed from fighting a virus or infection, or if you are emotionally stressed, an infusion of oatstraw can help soothe your nervous system. It's also high in calcium, antioxidants, and several other vitamins and minerals, while being a good source of soluble fiber. Place an ounce of chopped oatstraw in a quart-sized jar and pour boiling water over it. Cover and let it sit overnight. The next morning, strain it, and it will be ready for use. Store it capped in the refrigerator for no more than a week. Drink it as is, garnish with fruit, or use the liquid as a base for other drinks. You can use oatstraw fresh or dried. To dry, chop it roughly and lay flat on paper or clean cloth to air dry, as you would do with other herbs. Store completely dry oatstraw in a sealed jar away from sunlight.

A good all-around website for garden information is www .gardeningknowhow.com.

WHEAT

Wheat is another crop that you can plant in your garden space that will grow with little to no attention from you. Wheat likes to germinate in cool temperatures, so plant the wheat berries as soon as your ground is workable; that is, when hard frosts are past and you can actually get outside. Keep it watered (damp, not soggy!) and watch for germination. Harvest the wheat once the head is completely golden, with no hint of green. Test it by loosening a wheat berry and biting into it; if it's slightly chewy, it's not ready yet.

FLAX

Flax is one of the oldest domesticated crops. It has served to weave fine cloth, create rope, and produce oil. You can also add flaxseed whole or milled to your cooking and baking. It needs attention if you are growing it for quality or a specific use (such as oil or textiles), but otherwise it's fairly hardy. Like most other crops, flax is magically associated with prosperity and security.

One drawback to flax is that the straw doesn't decompose quickly or easily. It's a disadvantage only in the sense that it's not the best option if you're looking for a crop that can be plowed under or added to compost to enrich it. However, this durable, long-lasting quality is exactly what makes linen, the material spun from flax fiber, so useful. Examples of linen fabric have survived in graves from as long ago as 8,000 B.C.E., and threads found in other places even longer ago suggest that the use of flax to make fabric has an extremely long history.

GROUND COVER

Turf lawns aren't the most ideal way to cover ground. Ground cover needs to protect soil, resist weed intrusion, and be vigorous enough to fill the space relatively quickly and reliably. If tall, waving grains don't interest you, or if you want low-maintenance ground cover that doesn't require being cut down at the end of the growing season, look at planting clover or creeping thyme, depending on where you live. Options for slightly taller ground cover that flowers and doesn't need to be mown include creeping phlox, sweet woodruff (this makes a lovely strewing herb once dried), yellow alyssum (*Aurinia saxatilis*, not sweet alyssum), periwinkle (*Vinca minor*), pachysandra, and bunchberry (*Cornus canadensis*).

Chapter 7

Magic for a Healthy Garden

Charms for Tools and Equipment

Your garden tools are partners and players in your garden's well-being. You should treat your garden tools with the same kind of care you provide for your magical tools. In other words, cleanse them when you acquire them, purify them, and bless them before use (see Chapter 5). Dedicate them to your endeavor of husbandry. They are owed respect and gratitude. Check over your tools regularly to keep them in good shape. Look for nicks, scratches, and spots of rust. Treat them appropriately.

SPOKEN SPELL FOR CONNECTING TO YOUR TOOLS

When you prepare to use a tool, it can be useful to say a quick charm such as this one to focus what you're about to do and sync the tool's energy with your own.

(Name of tool), you and I are one.
You are an extension of myself.
We are focused, we are present.
May the work we do benefit this garden.
So may it be.

WHEN A TOOL BREAKS

Unlike ceremonial tools, gardening equipment sees heavy physical use. Sooner or later, something is going to break. When a tool is no longer useable—it breaks, the handle snaps, the blade is nicked badly enough that it can't be repaired with a sharpener, or some other way—thank it and magically decommission it. Cut the tie you formed with the tool by blessing, dedicating, and using it. Following is a quick ritual to help you do that. Dispose of the tool safely. If it can be dismantled or repurposed, go ahead and do so.

RITUAL

Releasing a Tool

It can feel awkward to throw something away when it was treated with respect when it came into your possession. This small ritual can be used to help. In place of the dish of soil, you can do the ritual outside in your garden, or inside in your garden space.

You'll Need: Matches or lighter • Votive candle or tea light in a holder • The tool • Small dish or glass of water • Small dish of soil

1 Center and ground. Light the candle.

2 Take up the tool. Say,

> *(Name of tool), you have been for me a helpmeet,*
> *Supporting my work of cultivation, nurturing, and care.*
> *Your part in this work is done.*
> *Thank you for your service.*
> *I release you.*

Breathe gently on the tool, and say,

> *By air, I release you.*

Pass the tool over the candle flame, and say,

> *By fire, I release you.*

Dip your fingers into the water and shake them onto the tool, and say,

> *By water, I release you.*

Finally, sprinkle the tool with a pinch of earth, or lay it on the ground, and say,

> *By earth, I release you.*

3 Close your eyes and imagine a tendril of energy connecting you and the tool. Raise a hand and bring it down through the tendril, visualizing it dissolving and fading away. Say,

> *(Name of tool), I release you.*
> *It is done.*

Magic for Garden Protection and Health

Magical protection for your garden is almost a given. As green witches, we want to protect and defend nature as best we can. In this instance, we're not defending the garden from abuse, we're defending it from things like disease, drought, and parasites.

There are different ways to go about this. First of all, work in the mundane world. That is to say, do all the right things that a non-witch would do: Make sure water levels, temperatures, soil quality, and other physical needs have been taken care of. Magic works with the path of least resistance. In other words, cross out anything that could threaten your garden's health as well as working magic. Magic and real-world action go hand in hand. Remember that physical activity in the world moves energy as well.

That said, there are different ways you can go about working protection for your garden.

A CHARM FOR WELCOMING NEW PLANTS

Bringing new plants into your garden is always an interesting experience. You have to think about how the new plant's energy will integrate into the garden's larger energy as a whole, as well as how it will interact with the plants in the area in which you intend to plant or place it. More than that, however, you have to think about what energy may be coming in that you hadn't planned on.

Just like when you add a new tool to your altar setup, it's a good idea to cleanse or purify plants you are bringing into the garden. You may be inclined to do this with decor, but it might not have occurred to you that a plant you bring home from the garden center or that is given to you by someone who split a plant in their own garden may carry energy from its

If you can, sense the energy of separate plants at the greenhouse or garden center when you are choosing specimens to bring home. This way, you will have a better sense of which one will fit in the best with your garden's overall energy, and you can pick the most appropriate one.

previous location with it. This energy may not be negative in any way, but you can't predict how it will interact with or affect your garden, so it's a good idea to clear whatever may be clinging to it so that the plant carries simply its own innate energies.

Just like cleansing a tool or stones and crystals, you can use various ways to cleanse a new plant of unwanted energy. If you enjoy working with stones and crystals, surround the plant with those that carry absorbent and/or purifying energy, such as smoky quartz, black tourmaline, and obsidian. If smoke cleansing is more your style, you can put together a quick blend of lavender, rosemary, and a pinch of thyme (or whatever your preferred herbs for purification are). Sprinkle the herbs on a lit charcoal tablet, and pass the heatproof dish holding it around the plant, wafting the smoke over and around the leaves, stem, and soil. If you're a water type of witch, you can make blessed water from your favorite recipe and mist the plant while visualizing unwanted energy evaporating from the leaves and fading away. You can use the remaining blessed water to water the plant.

> You can make a simple blessing water by steeping a sprig of lavender in a glass or bottle of water for a couple of hours and then straining it. You could also add or substitute a sprig of vervain. If you usually make blessed water by adding a pinch of salt, refrain from doing so here, as accumulated sodium in soil can be toxic to plants grown in it.

Sunlight is also an excellent purifier. If you have the time, and the plants don't have to be placed in the ground or repotted immediately, let them rest in a sunny place for a couple of days to release unwanted energy in their own time. If they are indoor plants, you might choose one of the previous methods instead so that the unwanted energy doesn't collect in your living space.

GENIUS LOCI

Genius loci is Latin for "spirit of place." In ancient Rome, a spirit of place was an entity of a specific location. A tutelary spirit was specifically protective. Historical imagery of a genius loci often includes

Establishing a spirit house in the spirit's preferred location is a way to make your relationship with the garden spirit more grounded. It's a lovely gesture to show the spirit how much you honor and appreciate it. See the Adding Magical Decor to Your Garden section later in this chapter for ideas.

symbols such as a cornucopia, a serpent, or a libation dish. It's considered a manifestation of the place itself, an aggregate of energy unique to that location that takes on awareness.

It's important to reach out to this spirit of place. Working in tandem with it for the good of the garden can be very rewarding, for it can help you understand the garden and interact with it on a deeper level.

How to best contact the genius loci? As always, this is a delicate meditation. Every spirit of place is different; you may get very clear impressions when you communicate with the spirit, or you may not. Stay confident and kind.

1. Sit quietly in the garden. Center and ground.
2. Open up your senses to the energies of the garden. In your own words, spoken or unspoken, invite the spirit of the garden to reach out to you.
3. Assure it that you have every intention of doing the best you can for the garden. Ask it to be the speaker for the garden. Promise to communicate with it regularly in order to stay on top of problems before they actually manifest; if you can head them off by following hints or suggestions from the spirit of the garden, so much the better.
4. Request it to formally take on the role of protector of the garden.
5. As thanks, make an offering to the spirit. Commit to doing this regularly. These can be left in a place you designate or that the spirit has indicated it would best like its representative spot to be.

OFFERINGS

An offering is a gesture of respect or thanks. This is done by sharing something with a spirit, deity, or familiar. In essence, it's a gift of energy. Often an offering is a libation (of water, a potion, or whatever beverage you were using as part of a ritual), food, or some other form of energy. Coins, crystals, incense, candles, handwritten or sketched thanks…all these represent a form of energy, given to a spirit of some kind. As regular thanks, small offerings can be made to the spirit of the garden. A larger offering after a specific working in the garden, or after harvest or planting, could be appropriate.

Let's take a moment to talk about offerings of herbs for garden spellwork or other magical purposes. It may feel odd to use plant matter in a spell designed to help your garden, especially plant matter gathered from that garden. Remember, however, that plants are part of a cycle that depends on decomposition, breaking down of organic matter into basic minerals, water, and elements that support future growth. An offering of plant matter makes perfect sense in this context.

CHARM AND SPELL TECHNIQUES FOR GARDEN MAGIC

Charms are small handcrafted spells hung or placed so that their energies can disseminate. There are many different ways to do this.

- **Charm bags** can be made from cloth (either a square of natural fabric gathered and tied shut or a cloth tea bag) and hung in the garden. These are designed to decompose over time, and will need to be replaced when they are worn through. You can remake the charm bag with the same materials and contents or make a different one.
- **Witch bottles** are a more permanent kind of charm. Materials are placed in a jar or bottle and sealed, then buried. They don't need to be large; we're not talking a 2-liter pickle jar. Tiny glass vials with plastic screw lids work perfectly well. If you can find tiny bottles with corks, you can use those and seal the corks closed with melted candle or sealing wax. Remember, it's not the quantity of spell materials you use; the energy and empowering you

It's good to have a stash of stone chips on hand, in a variety of crystals and stones, to add to charms like the ones in this section.

apply to the chosen supplies is more important. Try to avoid using jars or bottles with metal lids, as they will rust if used outdoors. Witch bottles can be buried in a central garden location, added to a spirit house to honor the spirit of the garden, or you can design bottles for specific purposes and bury them in associated areas (at the gate or other entrance to the garden, in a food-producing zone, in an area dedicated to healing herbs, and so forth). Witch bottles can also be used above ground, tied to stakes or trellises or containers, or displayed somewhere.

- **Bead charms** can be useful, and this is a technique I use often. Choose wooden beads for their color or a magical association of their wood (if you know it), or stone and crystal beads for their magical associations, and string them on hemp or linen cord. Make a small knot between each bead. Over time, the cord will decompose, allowing the beads to fall one by one. This doesn't end the charm; it just allows the stones, which have been charged by your intention as you crafted the charm, to shift their location.

- **Painted rocks** can be buried with plants or placed in a rock garden, under trees, or anywhere you like. We have rune stones painted with acrylics that are over ten years old in our garden, and they're still visible with little to no wear. Shellac is an eco-friendly finish that you can use without concern in a natural environment like your garden. You can use this method for creating protective garden stakes that identify the plants in the garden, as well. Paint runes or other protective symbols on the stones, add the plant names, then seal them and insert them in the soil by the appropriate plant or garden row.

If knot magic interests you, this is a great way to explore different patterns and styles while you work to knot your intention into the cord. You may be interested in reading *Knot Magic* by Tylluan Penry, or *Knot Magic* by Sarah Bartlett.

Another way to engage in magical protection in your garden is to bless the water to be used for watering the plants; this can be done by empowering the watering can, hose, and/or faucet you use to hook up your watering system. You can steep protective herbs in water, then strain and use the infusion to mist your plants. You can also asperse the garden.

Aspersing is the act of sprinkling something with blessed water to consecrate it. The easiest way to do this is to bless a cup or bowl of water, then dip your fingers in and sprinkle drops off the tips by flicking your hand. Blessing water can be as simple as holding your hands over it and charging it with your intent, bathing the water with energy charged with blessing. In this case, your intent would be to consecrate or bless something.

Aspersing can also unite water and earth. Steep dried or fresh herbs in water for at least three hours, then strain. Use this water to asperse the space. Or, you can use blessed water and dip stalks of fresh herbal matter into it, and shake droplets off the herb. Rosemary is particularly good for this. If you don't grow your own herbs or only have dried, supermarkets often sell stalks of fresh herbs in the produce section. Dip a stalk of your chosen herb into the water and use it to sprinkle drops around your chosen space.

Other good herbs to use as aspersers are fresh lavender, rosemary, or sage stalks.

Keep in mind that the materials you use in the garden for magic should be eco-friendly. A good material for garden magic is raffia, a string or rope-like material made from the raffia palm. The fiber is made from the membranes and underside veins of leaves; make sure the raffia you buy to use to tie up plants or for garden magic isn't artificial polypropylene or man-made raffia from wood pulp, which qualifies as viscose and is chemically treated in its production. True raffia, jute, and rough hemp are all natural materials that decompose without leaving microplastics or trash in the garden. Other ideas for magical elements to use in garden magic are corn husks, dried or damp, to fold around spell materials and tie closed with raffia, or willow branches, soaked then woven or bent and dried in that shape.

Garden Health

There are too many things that can go wrong in a garden, indoors or out, to list them all here. Mold in the soil, mites, overwatering, underwatering, incorrect soil acidity, unbalanced soil nutrients…a lot to juggle. Magic isn't the only thing you should do when there is a problem; your efforts should include work in the physical world as well. Assuming that you're pursuing practical solutions to your plant problems, ongoing magical work can supplement and reinforce your physical work.

In your work as a partner and protector of the earth, you might be interested in hosting bees on your property, if your situation allows it. It requires a lot of attention and work, and startup can be costly. You also need to operate within the laws of your state, region, or country, so be sure to research those thoroughly. There are beekeeper societies and groups everywhere, which are a great source of information, mentors, and support. Hosting bees is a wonderful way to give back to your garden.

One of the most important things you can do is check in daily with the spirit of your garden. It doesn't have to be a complex action, just a brief contact in order to recognize and greet it. If you have a spirit house, use that as your point of contact.

You can also do daily blessings or spoken charms throughout the day, at whichever times strike you or when you're active. You can also create blessings to be used at various points of the year, when specific things happen to your garden (when bulbs first break the ground, when the apple buds blossom, when the first leaf falls, and so forth). Here is a collection of spoken charms to inspire you.

DAILY BLESSING: MORNING

Morning light, bless this garden.
Bring it health and joy.
Guard it from shadow and ill intent.
So may it be.

DAILY BLESSING: EVENING

Plants actually grow faster at night. In daylight, they consume sunlight for photosynthesis, the process of which takes up energy. As photosynthesis can't take place at night, that energy goes toward growth instead.

Evening light, bless this garden.
May its growth be peaceful,
Strong, and confident.
May it grow true and sure.
So may it be.

SPRING BLESSING

Welcome, spring!
Bring fresh winds to blow away outdated thoughts and lingering fatigue.
May new light bring life to the particles of soil,
Gently waken the seeds,
And bless all that will grow here.

SUMMER BLESSING

Welcome, summer!
Rise high, sun, and let your glorious light fall
As precious nectar upon the land,
Like drops of gold, fertile energy.
Let it nourish the leaves and fruit.
May the summer rains be calm and quenching.
Grant this garden steady, healthy growth.

AUTUMN BLESSING

Welcome, autumn!
Golden light, cooler night,
Abundance and prosperity bless our gardens.
Thank you for your abundance,
For the vines and branches bending low with plenty.
May our harvests be fruitful.

WINTER BLESSING

Welcome, winter,
Season of reflection and repose.
Guide us as we turn inward to seek insight in the dark.
Remind us that the dark part of the cycle
Allows the soil to refresh,
Unneeded matter to return to its elemental parts.
Bless our fallow time,
And help us regenerate and use the transformational energy,
When again the time is right to seek the light of growth.
Grant us rest and rejuvenation.

COMPOST BLESSING

Compost has wondrous qualities that improve your garden soil in many ways. Use this blessing to focus and enhance its energy for maximum benefit.

Life turns to death,
And death turns beyond to deconstruct what once was life.
Return to your base elements,
Knowing your richness
Will become part of a future being.
This descent into darkness is a powerful transformation
And only by dying can we participate in life anew.
May this transformation be blessed,
And the rich yield create a better future.
So may it be.

SLEEP BLESSING

This is to be done when you are preparing the garden for the fallow season, whether that be winter, or whatever resting period you designate if your climate allows you to grow year-round.

Sleep, sleep.
Your work is done.
We have toiled together through sun and rain,
And now we rest.
Sleep safe,
Sleep secure,
Until you awaken in spring.
Be blessed in your respite.
So may it be.

You can also design a charm to protect your garden as it overwinters. What would you put in it? You might choose elements that are associated with sleep, protection, enrichment, peaceful rest, healing, and love. A combination of plants, stones, and anything else you want to include can work. You can choose to bury it, hang it somewhere near the spiritual center of the garden, or put it in your garden shrine or spirit house. When spring comes, undo the charm by either burning it (after removing what cannot burn) or composting it.

WASSAILING

Wassailing is an orchard fertility ritual. The word is presumed to come from the Old Norse *ves heill*, which became *weas haeil* in Middle English, meaning "be thou hale" or "be healthy."

The drink in question is a hot beverage of mulled cider and spices. Wassailing was the practice of sprinkling or pouring the beverage over the orchard trees to bring a plentiful harvest in the coming year, usually done on Twelfth Night. The trees are sung to, and there is often a procession going from orchard to orchard to bless them all. The practice is thought to scare away evil spirits who may be lurking to spoil the upcoming growing season, as well as to demonstrate the success of the previous harvest to the orchard.

Cider being the base for the drink isn't a fluke. Apples are associated with immortality, longevity, health, and love, and anyone whose orchard rested primarily on an apple crop would be keen to do all they could to ensure a good harvest in the upcoming year.

Create your own version of wassailing by making an infusion of herbs and greens from your garden, and offering it to the garden spirit in thanks for the year's harvest, and to protect the garden in the upcoming year.

Deities and Spirits Associated with Gardens

Gods and goddesses associated with horticulture are very common. Agriculture was an essential life-sustaining practice, so it makes sense that agrarian and harvest deities would figure largely in various cultures. There are generally more than one per cultural mythology, stemming from minor regional deities either being absorbed by or classified with a larger conquering culture's mythology. Japanese mythology has a class of spirits known as kami, and there are several agricultural-themed spirits among them. Here are a few deities associated with agriculture and horticulture:

> Weather gods also played an essential role in agrarian societies; this makes sense, as a farmer is very much at the mercy of the weather.

- **Demeter:** (Greek) The goddess of harvest and grain, as well as the cycle of life and death. Her iconography portrays her with fruit and grain, and the field poppy is one of her significant symbols.
- **Freyr:** (Norse) The twin of Freyja, Freyr is associated with peace, fertility, sun, good weather, and good harvests.
- **Ceres:** (Roman) The goddess of agriculture, grain crops, fertility. She is credited with teaching humanity about agriculture.

- **Hoori:** (Japanese) God of rice plants and fields, grain, and harvests.
- **Shujun/Shennong:** (Chinese) God of cultivation; he is said to have taught humans how to farm.
- **Inari Okami:** (Japanese) Kami (spirit) of rice, tea, agriculture, fertility, and foxes.
- **Osiris:** (Egyptian) God of agriculture, fertility, vegetation, and death.

Garden Folklore and Traditions

The amount of folklore that exists in relation to agriculture can be overwhelming when you start to look at it. Some of it is based on the belief that if something looks or behaves like a certain object or situation, then they must be related or linked in some sort of parallel way. In many cases, the protective folklore involves the concept of the harvest having a spirit or harvested material being linked to the land it grew on.

FIELD SPIRITS IN DIFFERENT CULTURES

In various cultures, it is believed that the corn spirit can take the form of an animal, such as a goose, fox, goat, or hare. The corn spirit would be trapped in the last bit of crop standing. What happens next depends on the local tradition. Some said the corn spirit had been trapped in the field after fleeing from the harvesters, and it is subsequently killed with the final stroke that harvests the final shock of grain. Or, the spirit was considered to be safely residing in the last bit of the crop, so it was carefully harvested and bound, then kept in a place of honor until the following planting season, when it was buried in the fields so that the spirit could move from the stored sheaf into the land again to bless the next crop. This sheaf could be called the corn mother or corn maiden.

Corn dollies are a form of art using the energy of the straw of the harvest, with some of the ears of grain as well. Wreaths, intricate shapes, and the like, they're not human forms; they often carry the connotation of protection or as favors to indicate affection.

The Butzemann is a different kind of protective figure, from the Dietsch (Pennsylvania Dutch) tradition. The Butzemann is a form of scarecrow, created in early February and stuffed with herbs and plants kept from the previous fall's harvest for this purpose. The spirits of the harvested plants are ritually invoked to animate the Butzemann, whose role is to protect the land, people, and buildings. In return, it requires a name and clothing, and offerings during the growing season. The Butzemann must be ritually burned to release its spirit by the last day of October, so that it is free to move on. If this is not done, the spirit leaves, but the body remains and can be inhabited by a malevolent spirit that can curse the fields and garden.

If you have an indoor garden or a container garden, you can make a miniature Butzemann. Honor it the way a large Butzemann is honored and burn it when it's time. If you have houseplants and don't grow plants that can be harvested, keep corn husks as you eat fresh corn, and add herbs you've purchased, cleansed, and dried for this purpose. Remember to use natural materials like cotton or linen, so that it burns easily and without noxious smoke.

Other protective measures are statues empowered to defend the garden, small mirrors to redirect or reflect bad fortune, hanging glass balls known as witch balls to trap negative energy or evil spirits, and wind chimes or small bells to break up negative energy. A common sight in gardens is a face of the Green Man, a protective spirit associated with vegetation and growing things.

Magical Tips for Caring for Your Garden

If you're in North America, one of the most important aids you can pick up is a copy of the current *Old Farmer's Almanac*, or bookmark the *Old Farmer's Almanac* website at www.almanac.com. If you pick up a physical copy, make sure you get the one that's written for your country, as the predictions and growing seasons vary by location.

Science has come a long way, and meteorologists can predict what kind of winter we'll have by examining trends and comparing them to models and projections. But before we had that kind of science available, people relied on the *Old Farmer's Almanac* to know when to plant, harvest, and interact with the expected growing season.

The *Old Farmer's Almanac* focuses on living by the rhythms of nature, not the calendar. It also offers folklore from various areas, moon rise and set times, moon phases, astronomical activity like meteor showers, projected frost dates, gardening tips, seasonally related crafts and activities, and articles on a variety of topics. They also have a kids' version available at www.almanac.com/kids.

Gardening by the Moon

We discussed the impact the moon can have on gardening in Chapter 3, but here's a reminder of the general guidelines regarding gardening activity throughout the moon phases.

- **New to first quarter:** plant leafy annuals and herbs
- **First quarter to full:** plant flowering annuals, aboveground vegetables and fruit, and vines
- **Full to third quarter:** plant perennials, root vegetables, and bulbs
- **Third quarter to dark:** weed, maintain, cultivate, and fight pests and disease.

Surprise Plants

At some point, every gardener discovers an uninvited plant growing somewhere in their garden. Uninvited doesn't mean unwelcome, of course; it just means it's a surprise. Maybe a tiny seed hitched a ride in the soil of a new potted houseplant. Perhaps squirrels dug up bulbs from somewhere else and used your garden as a hiding spot. The wind spreads airborne seeds and pollen, while bird and animal dung can contain the seeds of fruits or other plants eaten elsewhere and deposited on your property. Nature is efficient, and very good at making sure things have the best possible chance of survival by widening the territory covered. Surprise plants are like volunteers for your garden.

This is both miraculous and frustrating to a gardener. On one hand, nature is wondrous! And on the other, you can work hard to make sure a plant stays alive, only to have it fade away for no discernible reason; meanwhile, weeds or surprise plants thrive.

Weeds are impressive plants. They're stubborn and strong, and flourish wherever they please. Often, that's where we don't want them to grow, having marked out that space for specific other plants. However, weeds are negative only because of where they pop up. If you look at what society considers weeds—dandelions, chickweed, plantain, self-heal, cleavers, stinging nettle—these plants are often used in herbal medicine. They're stubborn and strong and common because they're useful and beneficial. They don't exist to annoy gardeners; they exist to help humanity.

Surprise plants are like gifts or omens. Try to identify it, first of all, if it isn't immediately recognizable to you. Look it up and read about the associated lore. Is it considered a healing plant? Is it associated with protection, storms, specific animals? What superstitions surround it? Then look at where it appeared. Near a door? In an unused portion of your garden space? What other plants are nearby? What time of year did it show up?

Looking at all these factors can help you form an idea of what meaning might be attached to the appearance of the plant. I'll walk you through my process of handling a surprise plant. Last summer, I found a single white columbine growing under our back deck, and asked my partner if he'd planted it. He hadn't; we've never planted columbines. I hadn't seen any in gardens around us either. We identified it using https://identify.plantnet.org, and I looked up folklore and historical uses of columbines. One of my favorite sources for this is *Culpeper's Complete Herbal*. He let me down a bit, though:

These are so well known, growing almost in every garden, that I think I may save the expense of time in writing a description of them.

Really, Culpeper?

But he came through later in the entry:

The leaves of columbines are commonly used in lotions with good success for sore mouths and throats; Tragus saith, that a drachm of the seed taken in wine with a little saffron, openeth obstructions of the liver, and is good for the yellow-jaundice, if the party after the taking thereof be laid to sweat well in his bed; the seed also taken in wine causeth a speedy delivery of women in child-birth: if one draught suffice not, let her drink a second, and it will be effectual. The Spaniards use to eat a piece of the root hereof fasting, many days together, to help them when troubled with the stone in the reins or kidneys.

So columbine is good for liver and kidney function. It works as a diuretic on the organs that work to purify. It was used to soothe mouths and throats; these are used for communication, as well as taking in nourishment. Speeding up childbirth can be considered bringing something to fruition or production.

What about medical uses more modern than the 1650s? In *A Modern Herbal* ("modern" here being 1931) Mrs. Grieve tells us that columbine is an astringent, but it is no longer used because overdose is toxic. (Mrs. Grieve also does a good job of describing the plant, taking eight paragraphs to do it. Thank you, Mrs. Grieve.) She also mentions that the botanical name, *Aquilegia vulgaris*, comes from the Latin word *aquila*, meaning "eagle," and the Saxon name for it was "culverwort" (*culfer* being the word for "pigeon"), while *columb* is Latin for "dove." It is therefore associated with birds, one a predator and the other a peace- and love-associated bird (doves and pigeons are very closely related, and can be grouped together for our purposes).

A quick toxicity check says that all parts of the plant are poisonous if ingested. Sorry, Culpeper; we're going with Mrs. Grieve on this. (Also, this is why you always check more recent material instead of doing something because an old book said it was okay to do.)

The color of the columbine we found was white, and although more commonly they are various shades of purple. The corner of the back deck marks the end of the walk-through space between the house and the side fence, just before the yard opens up and the vegetable garden begins.

Taking all this information and sorting through it, I get purification from the Culpeper information and the color white, freedom from the bird association, and the location suggests both support (it was right next to the post that the corner of the back deck rests on) and shifting from utilitarian space to a more relaxed area. I could connect the vegetable garden and the Culpeper mention of the mouth and throat and thereby tie in food, but it doesn't feel right to me.

Therefore, the takeaway from this surprise columbine for me is that it brings a message of moving past challenges, growing or emerging out of a period or situation of making do into a more promising, supportive time or situation that offers more freedom, allowing us to shed negative or not-ideal things that were holding us back or dragging us down.

Typing all this out and looking back at exactly when we noticed the columbine…it did indeed foreshadow just that for our family. At the time, we had no idea what was coming. This is a great example of why reviewing your notes, journaling, and research on a regular basis is important; what seems vague at the time can make a lot more sense later.

Amplifying the Magic of Your Ingredients

The concept of companion planting in agricultural practice is an interesting one. It posits that when certain plants are set next to one another, they can improve their overall general health as well as their yields. For example, planting nasturtiums among your vegetables reduces the damage aphids can do, because the nasturtiums draw the aphids to them. Other companion planting practices are common sense, such as planting leafy vegetables such as spinach in the shade of taller plants. In many companion planting pairs, the plants draw different kinds of nutrients or minerals from the soil, so they're non-competitive.

We can bring this to a magical parallel: What can we plant together to strengthen the magical outcome? What complements certain other plants?

Choose areas for specific purposes (e.g., protection) and plant a single one of each plant you intend to use for protection magic. The same plants may appear elsewhere in your garden but with different aspects of their energies to bring out: happiness, healing, prosperity, and so forth. Plants have more than one magical correspondence, after all. Growing lavender in separate enhancement zones can strengthen different aspects of its energy. Think of how we encode intention when we use an herb in magic, calling on a specific aspect of its energy. This is what we're doing here, but from the ground up.

There's a reverse side to all this as well. Certain plants don't like to grow near one another at all. Onions and garlic tend to hold peas and beans back from performing their best, and despite both being brassicas, cauliflower and cabbage are cranky when planted together.

On a magical level, think about the challenge an herb planted for attraction might have growing next to an herb you're cultivating specifically for returning unwanted energy whence it came. Plant similar or complementary herbs being grown for specific purposes together.

Adding Magical Decor to Your Garden

Enhancing your garden area with symbolic and aesthetically pleasing decor is a wonderful way to express yourself, and to enhance certain aspects of your garden's energy.

ELEMENTAL DECOR

Having representative symbols of the four elements is a lovely way to honor them and invite their blessings into your garden space.

A small water feature or birdbath can represent water. If your water symbol doesn't have moving water (like a birdbath), make sure to clean it out regularly to avoid buildup of leaves and dirt. Stagnant water can be a breeding ground for mosquitoes too. Flowing water features don't have to be large installations, either. They can be as simple as a sub-mersible pump in a flower pot, or an aquatic garden in a decorative container.

A fire bowl, pit, or lantern can represent fire. There are smaller, tabletop gas-powered fires available now, if a full fire pit isn't possible. However, I cannot stress enough how important it is to check your civic bylaws to see what the rules are concerning open flames and semi-permanent installations on your property. Solar lanterns or garden lights are a safer way to add the energy of fire to your garden; they gather energy from the sun to charge their power cells. Candles can be lovely, but they require close supervision if you're using them for spellwork.

You may think there isn't much point in placing a symbol of earth in a garden, but selecting something specific to represent it provides a focus and honors the element. A statue or specially selected stone can represent earth. Crystals placed in corners of garden beds or hung in tree branches are another lovely way to bring the energy of earth into your garden.

Air can be evoked by wind chimes, flags, or pinwheels.

SHRINES AND ALTARS

These two terms are often substituted for one another, but there is a difference. An altar generally means a physical space used for magical work or worship. A shrine is generally a specific site set up to honor an entity or principle.

What to use in your garden is up to you. If you would like to create a relatively permanent magical workspace in your garden, try placing a rock with a relatively flat surface somewhere, or designate a small wicker table as a portable altar. If you do a lot of potting work or cutting and rooting, a potting table set somewhere for magical and mundane activity could serve well.

Shrines can be permanent or temporary. See the next section for a shrine for the spirit of the garden. Temporary shrines can be made if you're working with a specific spirit or deity for a particular short-term purpose. Remember that outdoor shrines will be subject to the weather, so choose appropriate materials, or factor the eventual breakdown of the materials into the shrine itself.

SPIRIT HOUSES

A spirit house is a dwelling created specifically for the spirit of a place. In Asia, spirit houses are common; they range in size from small roofed house-like structures on the ground or on pillars to elaborate structures large enough to walk into. In some cases they are places for troublesome spirits to stay so that people won't be bothered, but in others they house protective spirits. Offerings are left at these spirit houses to either bribe or thank the spirits.

Once you have made contact with the spirit of your garden, ask it if it has a preferred location for where it would like its representative place to be. Think of this as the spirit's "home base," a place for it to live. A spirit house gives you the opportunity to have a consistent, physical location for offerings and communication with the spirit of the garden.

ARBORS

Arbors are arched or lintel-shaped trellises. Arches are magical things. They represent moving from one state to another, a liminal moment on a journey. Arbors have trelliswork on the side supports. This represents support in growth and expansion.

GATES

Gates are another liminal space, but with the door they can also represent protection. Doors can symbolize holding something in for safety, keeping things out for protection, or a signal that a conscious change is being made as you open and step through. A gate or door is a very powerful thing.

STATUARY

Statues are a form of art that is often featured in gardens. Made of weather-resistant materials, they can be decorative or symbolic. Angels, fairies, and deities are common; gnomes, animals, and magical creatures can add a different sort of energy, or be guardians. Architectural statuary such as pillars, spheres, or benches can all support magical intention in various places as well.

Garden art like glass or metal flowers can add whimsy, or be empowered for specific goals related to their colors or shapes.

Chapter 8

Make Magic with Your Harvest

Cooking with Produce from Your Garden

Working with your garden's harvest can be both a form of magical blessing and an expression of gratitude for that harvest. The magic you can work with your garden's bounty has almost no limits. Magic can be performed as you harvest, during food preparation, or when serving the food. You can perform different kinds of magic at all three steps, if you like.

FRUIT

Fruit can be eaten out of hand, of course, but if you want to use it magically, there are several ways you can involve it.

- Use fruit juice as blessing liquid in rituals and spells.
- Put together a fruit salad and eat it mindfully, taking the time to think about the magical energy contained within each bite as you consume it. Visualize that energy merging with yours.
- Make a pie, selecting the fruit for your desired magical goal. Draw symbols supporting your magical goal on the top crust. If the pie doesn't have a top crust, draw it on the bottom crust with a toothpick or lay thin strips of pie dough in the bottom crust in your desired shape before you pour in the fruit filling.

MAKING JAM MAGICALLY

The process of making jam offers several opportunities to visualize magical goals. The very act of thickening the fruit compote until it gels is a terrific metaphor for a spell coming together to create a new version of reality. Transformation is a key concept in kitchen magic, and jam is an excellent ingredient to use for making magic with food. You can select the fruits to support your magical goal, empower the mixture with your intention while you stir, and visualize the goal coming into reality as the jam gels. Consume the jam to reinforce your intention or use it for general sweetness and abundance.

There's a complex art to making jam, involving pectin levels, proportion of sugar to fruit, and thermometers. If you're making a huge batch of jam, then I recommend reading up on the process to get a better handle on it so that you don't end up tossing an entire batch of jam that has gone wrong. This recipe, however, makes a tiny amount—just a cup or two—and is a great way to try making jam if you've never done it before. Likewise, I wouldn't can a large batch of jam in this way, but for a small amount that will be eaten within a month or shared among friends, it's fine.

You'll Need:
- 4 cups roughly chopped fruit
- Juice of 1 medium lemon
- ½ cup granulated sugar
- 2 (1-cup) Mason jars, sterilized
- New sealing lids and rings, sterilized
- Labels

What to Do:
1. Place the fruit, lemon juice, and sugar in a medium-sized saucepan with a heavy bottom. Stir and cook it over medium heat until the mixture begins to bubble.
2. Reduce heat to low and stir. Allow the mixture to simmer gently, stirring every 15 minutes or so, and watch the fruit break down. Increase the frequency of your stirring as the jam begins to thicken, and pay attention so it doesn't burn or thicken past your desired consistency.
3. Pour the hot jam into the clean and sterilized jars. Wipe the rim of the jars with a damp clean cloth to remove any spills. Place the seal on the rim and screw on the lid.
4. Leave the jars where they won't be disturbed and allow the natural cooling process to make the seal. If the jars don't seal, keep them in the refrigerator before opening.
5. Label the jars clearly with the date and magical information.

HERBS

There may be a time when you want to harvest herbs at a particular time for the astrological correspondence with the moment of harvesting (such as planetary hours, moon phase, or the daily solar cycle). The timing of the correspondence might not match the time when you want to work with the herbs, however. What should you do?

If you can use your harvested plant dry, then just hang it somewhere where it can dry out. If you want to use it fresh, however, and your intended use isn't more than a few days away, here are some tips:

- Loosely wrap herbs in a damp paper towel, then seal in a zip-top plastic bag filled with air. Refrigerate up to five days. Check the herbs daily, as some of them lose their flavor after a couple of days.
- Store herbs bouquet-style when in bunches: Place, stems down, in a jar with water covering one inch of the stem ends, enclose in a large zip-top plastic bag, and change the water every other day. Most herbs will keep for up to a week this way. To revive limp herbs, trim a half an inch off the stems, and place in ice water for a couple of hours.
- Wash herbs just before using; pat dry with a paper towel.

Herbs have a very different flavor profile when fresh as compared to when they're dry. The flavor is concentrated after the water in the leaves and stems has evaporated. This is why measurements for fresh herbs call for more than recipes calling for dried.

My other books offer plenty of recipes and projects for using herbs to make vinegars and oils, so instead of those options, we're going to look at a couple of simple ways to incorporate your herbal harvest into cooking in a different way—by making herbal butter and salt. Herbal butter and herbal salt can be used in cooking and baking, thereby adding a bit of your harvest and the energies of the herbs you used in creating them to whatever you make.

Herbal Butter

Herb butter can be added to vegetables, melted and drizzled over meat or popcorn, or spread on bread. It is easy to make and keeps for about two months in the fridge or six months in the freezer, well wrapped.

When choosing your herbs, keep their magical properties in mind as well as their flavors. Empower the herbal mix before you add it to the butter. Dairy carries a base energy of nurturing and healing energy, so that will be part of the end product as well. Vegan butter works just as well, though the magical energies will be slightly different. Vegan butter often has coconut and soy as the main ingredients; the magical associations of coconut are protection and purification, while soy is associated with protection and psychic awareness.

The basic proportions are 1–3 teaspoons of chopped herbs to ½ cup of softened butter. Put the butter in a bowl and mash it with a fork, then add the chopped herbs and mash some more. When well mixed, scrape it out onto a square of waxed paper in a roughly log-like shape, and roll the paper up, firming the log as you do. Twist the ends to seal and refrigerate until firm.

Herbal Salt

Seasoned salt adds so much more flavor than plain salt! This, too, is lovely sprinkled over vegetables or meat. As with herbal butter, choose your herbs for their magical associations as well as their flavors, and empower them with your magical goal before mixing.

You'll Need:
- 1 cup kosher salt, sea salt, or other coarse salt
- 3–5 teaspoons finely chopped fresh herbs (remove woody stems)
- 1 teaspoon freshly ground black pepper
- 1 teaspoon lemon zest
- 2 teaspoons lemon juice

What to Do:

1. Preheat oven to 200°F.
2. In a medium bowl, combine all ingredients, stirring thoroughly so that the mixture blends evenly.
3. Spread the mixture evenly onto a parchment-lined baking sheet.
4. Bake salt 30–45 minutes, checking regularly. Stir every 15 minutes to allow the herbs to dry evenly.
5. Remove when the salt looks dry. Allow it to cool, then use a fork to gently break up any clumps. Store in a sealed container.

BOUQUET GARNI

The bouquet garni (literally "garnished bouquet") is a classic herb blend used to flavor foods. The traditional blend is bay leaf, parsley, and thyme, but many people have developed their own combinations and use them as a signature blend. The traditional blend carries energy of courage, healing, strength, purification, and banishing negativity.

Why bundle the bouquet garni? Sometimes you don't want bits of herbs floating around, and when sprigs of fresh herbs cook for a long time they don't look very appetizing. If you're looking for a particular presentation, bundling can help.

If your herbs are fresh from your garden, you can bundle them together and wrap them with kitchen string, adding them to the base for your dish and removing them before serving. If you've dried your garden herbs, the easiest way to use them is to put them in the center of a square of muslin or cheesecloth, and tie it shut with kitchen string. Add it to your base and remove the bundle before serving.

FREEZING HERBS IN OIL

If you want to use your garden herbs fresh rather than drying them for future use, then try chopping them roughly, covering them with olive oil, and freezing them in ice-cube molds. You then have an easy way to start a meal in a warm pan or to add flavor to a soup or stew. You can freeze single herbs in the oil, or make blends for specific purposes,

Herbes de Provence makes a great dried herb blend too. It's best to grind it, either with a mortar and pestle or a spice grinder, so that the size difference between the various ingredients is minimized.

such as chopped garlic, basil, and oregano for tomato sauce; rosemary and thyme for potatoes; or an herbes de Provence–type blend for all-purpose cooking. There are many recipes for herbes de Provence, but the majority include some combination of thyme, savory, oregano, rosemary, marjoram, basil, tarragon, parsley; some include lavender, fennel, or bay leaf.

SAVORY SHORTBREAD

If you've never had savory shortbread, you're in for a treat. Use your garden-fresh herbs for this recipe, so they're fragrant; and chop them finely with a sharp knife. These are lovely to add to cheese plates, serve with soups, or just to nibble on. You can use your favorite shortbread recipe, and try substituting herbs and cheese for the sugar. Or, if using the following recipe, you'd add the chopped herbs to the dough along with the flour. Play with the proportions; shortbread has few ingredients and is easily scaled up or down. The great thing about this is that it's easy to make a small batch for testing, and you can taste the dough along the way.

If you don't have a shortbread recipe, this is a very easy one for a small batch. Scale it up or down as you desire. It yields approximately 12–16 cookies, depending on the size of your cookie cutters.

You'll Need:
- ½ cup butter, at room temperature
- ¼ cup powdered sugar, sifted
- 1 cup all-purpose flour, sifted

What to Do:
1. Preheat the oven to 350°F.
2. In a medium mixing bowl, cream the butter and sugar together until light and fluffy.

3. Add the flour and mix until the dough comes together.
4. On a floured surface, roll out the dough to ½" thick. Use cookie cutters to cut out shapes, or a knife to cut into squares. Transfer cookies to a lightly greased baking sheet, spacing them about ¾" apart, and refrigerate for 15 minutes. (Alternatively, roll the dough into a 2½"-wide log, wrap in plastic wrap, and refrigerate for 30 minutes; use a sharp knife to cut ½" slices, place them on the baking sheet, and proceed.)
5. Remove the baking sheet from the refrigerator and place in oven. Bake 15–18 minutes, or until edges are golden brown. Allow cookies to cool slightly before transferring them to a cooling rack.

Savory shortbread is also an excellent way to use an herb butter (see earlier in this chapter). Here are suggestions for flavor combinations:

- Thyme and lemon
- Basil and orange
- Lemon, black pepper, and Asiago cheese
- Rosemary and Parmesan cheese
- Chives and Cheddar cheese

Wassail is a traditional drink akin to mulled wine that was drunk and poured at the roots of orchard trees to bless them and ensure good harvest later in the year. Wassailing is a form of garden magic. Why not try your own recipe or modify an existing one to use produce from your own garden? See Chapter 7 for more on wassail.

MULLING SPICES

Traditional mulling spices (cinnamon, cloves, star anise, and so forth) are usually not growable in private gardens in the Northern Hemisphere; they require a very specific climate and environment. This means that you can think about what you can add to the blend that does grow in your garden, an addition to enhance the mix and personalize it.

VEGETABLES

Using vegetables in magic may seem unusual. However, harvest in general revolves around celebrating success, food security, and the magic of growth. It's a time to express gratitude for nature's bounty, and thanks for the relationship we have with nature that enables us to reflect on the spiritual harvests in our own lives.

MIREPOIX

Mirepoix is a savory base for many dishes and sauces. Diced onions, carrots, and celery are cooked slowly over low heat in fat (butter and/or oils). The vegetables aren't intended to caramelize; the goal is to create a sweet and concentrated flavor.

The mirepoix also combines very specific magical energies, if you choose to use it that way. Onions both clear negative energy and promote healing. Carrots are also associated with health and fertility. Celery carries magical energies of love, peace, and concentration. With all these, you can empower your mirepoix for a variety of things, enhancing specific combinations. For example, if you are struggling with anxiety, you can invoke the onion's healing, the carrot's grounding, and the celery's peace. If you are trying to conceive (physically or creatively), use the onion's banishing of negative energy, the carrot's fertility, and the celery's love and concentration.

> This kind of fine-tuning of magical associations and inherent energies of ingredients is a subtle but very effective way to use them for a variety of magical goals. Try this exercise: Sit down with your favorite recipes and look at the ingredients, then consider their magical associations. How many different magical goals can you come up with for the same recipe, just by emphasizing different aspects of the energy correspondences?

There are various cultural versions of mirepoix (the Italian soffritto comes to mind, as does the Creole "holy trinity" of onion, carrot, and green bell pepper), but the traditional French version has two parts onion, one part carrot, and one part celery.

VEGETABLE SOUP

One of the easiest ways to make magic in the kitchen is to make vegetable soup. It's warm, filling, and vegan. Best of all, you can use whatever vegetables you have on hand, and it can turn out differently as you make it throughout the harvest season, depending on what vegetables are available. It begins with a mirepoix, so you can build on that magical base.

This recipe calls for two cups of vegetables, but that may not even make a dent in your bounty! Anything goes here: zucchini, tomatoes (peel them first), peas, green beans, potatoes, corn, sweet potatoes, bell peppers, squash…whatever is in your garden.

> If you want to add greens such as kale or spinach, don't add them with the other vegetables; add them about 5 minutes before you remove the soup from the heat.

You'll Need:

- 3 tablespoons olive oil
- 1 medium onion, chopped
- 2 large carrots, peeled and chopped
- 2 stalks celery, chopped
- 2 cups chopped vegetables (see earlier note)
- Salt, to taste
- 4 cloves garlic, chopped (or to taste)
- ½ teaspoon dried thyme (or 1 teaspoon fresh thyme)
- 2 cups tomato juice
- 5 cups vegetable broth
- Freshly ground black pepper, to taste
- 1 bay leaf
- Zest of 1 medium lemon

What to Do:

1. Heat the olive oil in a large saucepan over medium heat. Add the onions, carrots, celery, and chopped vegetables. Add salt. Cook, stirring often, until the onion is soft and translucent, about 5–8 minutes.

2. Add garlic and thyme. Cook while stirring for about 1 minute.

3. Add the tomato juice and cook 4–5 minutes longer.

4. Add the vegetable broth. Season with more salt and freshly ground black pepper, and add the bay leaf.

5. Adjust heat to high and bring the soup to a boil, then cover and reduce the heat to low to simmer gently for about 20 minutes.

6. Remove lid and stir. (If you are using chopped greens this is when you would add them.) Cook for 5 more minutes.

7. Remove from heat and stir in the lemon zest. Taste and adjust the seasoning to your preference.

8. If you have leftovers, this soup freezes very well.

Divination with Your Garden

If you're a bird lover, a container or outdoor garden can be a wonderful location to practice some form of divination based on the kinds of birds you see, where you see them, how many you see, or what they're doing. My book *The Hidden Meaning of Birds* may interest you, as it looks at the energies and meanings associated with various birds; you can combine this with your knowledge of the magical energies associated with the plants you grow and use your intuition to interpret the information.

If you're familiar with the *I Ching* system of divination, you may know that the sticks originally used were yarrow stems. Nature has often been a source of information that people have sought to use as oracles or ways to predict what might come in the future.

INTUITIVE DIVINATION

One of the easiest ways to use your garden for guidance or divination is to do it intuitively. Listening to nature is probably already something you do as a witch. Taking it a step further to use your garden space as a form of guidance or foretelling is a natural choice.

Prepare in whatever way you are inspired to prepare. Spiritual bath or shower? Smoke cleansing? If you want to prepare in the garden, maybe you want to set up a candle and incense or however you set up for meditations. Before you begin, make sure you have your question clear in your mind.

1. Settle yourself in your garden however you like; whether that be by sitting in a chair, cross-legged on the ground, or lying down on a blanket.
2. Center and ground, then hold your question in your mind.
3. When you feel ready, clear your mind and open yourself to the energy of the garden and any messages it might have for you.

CREATING A GARDEN ORACLE DECK

Oracle decks aren't prescriptive; instead, they offer you ideas and concepts to consider, allowing you to use intuition and reflection to come to your own meaning. Creating a garden-based oracle deck allows you to design a very specific tool unique to you and your associations with various plants and features of your own garden. How you do it is a very personal process; the following are only suggestions:

1. Begin by drawing or taking photos of different plants in your garden. Print out photos on 4" × 6" blank postcards or matte photo paper. If you have sketched them, color your drawings.
2. Look in your grimoire or other personal research for what each plant means in lore, or what its magical correspondences are. Make a short list of keywords associated with the plant in your practice. You can write the keywords on the card or keep them on a separate list.

> Remember, your associations with the plant are more important than ones listed in books. Books are great places to start, but don't stop there.

3. Start a notebook devoted to your oracle deck. Devote a single page or a double-page spread to each plant card. Write as much as you like about it: traditional associations, your personal associations, all the keywords you came up with for it. Add a copy of the card itself, if you like.

4. Use the rest of the notebook to record your divination sessions with the oracle. See the following for suggested methods you can use for those sessions.

Here are some further ideas:

≈ Write a poem about the plant to add to the card.

≈ Instead of using a photo or sketch, make a collage.

≈ Press a sprig of the plant, glue it to the card, then laminate it.

≈ Use patterned paper on the reverse of the card to make the deck cohesive and attractive.

Here are some ideas for how to use your unique garden oracle deck:

≈ Draw a card first thing in the morning to give you a concept to think about during the day.

≈ Draw a card at bedtime and keep the keyword(s) in mind as you drift off to sleep. Journal any dreams or insights when you awaken.

≈ For a meditation session, draw a card and envision the plant before you. Envision your energy reaching forward to mingle with that of the plant.

≈ Do a standard three-card layout. Place three cards in a row in front of you, face down. The first gives insight into where you've come from; the second offers insight into your current situation; the third suggests a direction to go in.

Using What You've Grown in Witchcraft

Your garden can be a valuable source of material for magical tools and supplies. As a green witch, this is probably one of the goals you had in mind when you planned your garden. I have provided many different ways of using harvested herbs and plants in my previous books, so I won't repeat it all here. Instead, I'm going to provide you with some basic proportions for suggested projects.

MAKING YOUR OWN WANDS

To make a wand, gather together the stems of some of your garden herbs. Soak your selected stems in water to soften them, then braid them, fasten them together, and dry. You can make different wands from different plants depending on your magical goals. You can save your wand to use over and over, or you can burn it at the end of your spell as an offering or to seal the spell/declare it complete once your goal is achieved.

If you'd like to make home-made paper for use in spell casting, see *The Green Witch's Grimoire* for instructions. Instead of using flower petals, you can use a powdered blend of selected herbs to support your magical goal. Or you can sprinkle seeds onto the wet paper before pressing it, then cut it up into smaller pieces and use them to sow.

HERBAL WREATHS

Herbal wreaths are a lovely way to use harvested herb matter from your garden. Choose plants according to your magical goals, and when you harvest them make sure you cut them as close to the main stem or root as you can. Begin arranging the stems in a row in a line, placing the head or top of each sprig just below the previous one. As you go, wrap the stems around each other or bend them to help keep them together. You can also use raffia to help keep them together, wrapping it around the stems and the heads of the sprigs. Begin curving the line of stems down and around, until you overlap with the beginning stem.

Fasten it either by tucking the head between two of the earlier stems or by tying it. Hang it or keep it wherever you want the energies to work.

An easier version is to create a small flat bouquet or posy of the herbs, the stems braided together and fastened with raffia or cotton string. The circular wreath shape carries the connotation of cycles and unity, however, which is why I prefer to use it. When the magical use for the herbal wreath is complete, compost the plant material.

BOTANICAL WATERS

There are two different kinds of botanical waters: the kind you can drink, and the kind you can't. Those that you cannot drink can be used as potions. You can use these to mist plants or spaces or bottle them and place them in areas that you wish to affect with the energy contained therein. The following is a recipe for an infused botanical water intended to be consumed:

You'll Need:
- ½ cup clean, chopped plant matter
- Cloth tea bag or infuser
- Jar large enough for the water and plant matter
- 1 quart of filtered water

What to Do:
1. Place the chopped plant matter in a cloth bag or a removable infuser, such as the kind used for ice tea.
2. Place the container of plant matter in a large jar with a lid, and pour the water over it. Place in the sun for 1–3 hours.
3. Strain and transfer to a jug or bottle and keep in the refrigerator for a maximum of one week.

Different plant matter can require different lengths of time to infuse properly. Using heat can speed up the process, such as with making an infusion for tea, but if you are looking to make a straight water that is infused as opposed to making a tea-type of potion, you may have to do some experimentation. Some fruits and heavier plant matter will require longer steeping time, whereas others may become bitter if steeped too long. Taste the water at regular intervals in order to stop when it has reached a flavor you enjoy. Always remember to strain out the plant matter, however, or it can become slimy, and that makes your resulting infusion rather unappetizing.

Drinking infused botanical waters can be very refreshing in the summer, and a lovely way to involve the energy of herbs and plants and fruit in an easily prepared fashion. Try the following combinations:

- Lime and melon
- Ginger and mint
- Cucumber and basil
- Lemon and blueberry

Botanical infusions intended for magical use that don't involve drinking them can be made with any plant, flower, or fruit of your choice. Label the container clearly as magical potion only, not to be consumed. Any infused water should be kept in the refrigerator. Dispose of the water after one week, even if it isn't intended to be consumed. You can dispose of it respectfully by pouring it outdoors by your magical workspace, altar area, offering space, or spirit house.

> Lustral water, a simple blessing water, is made by placing a spring of vervain in water.

You can make floral waters in a similar way, by steeping clean flower petals in water. If the flowers are not toxic in any way, you can use this kind of floral water to add to baths, facial misting, hair rinse, and so on.

INFUSED OILS

Basically, to make an infused oil you will fill a quart-sized Mason jar with botanical material. Leave about two inches free at the top. Slowly fill the jar with your chosen oil, then close and allow it to steep for two to three weeks, shaking the bottle at least once daily. When the oil has the fragrance you're looking for, strain the botanical material out and place the oil in a new clean bottle with a lid. Label it with the date and contents and record any additional magical information in your garden journal or grimoire. Kept in a dark place, an infused oil should keep up to one year.

Like potions, oils can be consumable or non-consumable depending on what botanical matter you used for your chosen magical purpose. Some plants can be used in a topical application, even if they shouldn't be consumed; others should only be used for magical purposes and not for body care.

MAGICAL TOOLS

There are many ways for you to use things from your garden in creating magical tools. Try the following:

- Look into making your own paper for spellwork, and use material from your garden in the mix. You can use ground dried herbs or dried petals, or add a pinch of soil from a specific place in your garden that carries specific energies, for example. (For instructions on how to make your own paper, see *The Green Witch's Grimoire*.)

- You can use branches from trimmed shrubs or trees as wands or staffs, or as magical and physical stem support for smaller plants. Choose them for their magical correspondences or for personal associations. Forked sticks or small branches can be used as stangs, which can be used as working altars, shrines, or vehicles for spellwork in the garden. (For more on stangs, see Chapter 5.)

- Rainwater is a useful item to have on hand for spellwork. Use a clean container to catch it; fasten a piece of cheesecloth or muslin over the top with an elastic band to keep dirt and foreign objects out while it is collecting rainwater. Decanted into a small bottle and labeled, rainwater can be kept in the refrigerator for a couple of weeks. You can catch rainwater during specific storms for immediate or imminent use. If you want to keep storm water or rainwater collected at a specific time (such as during a specific moon phase, full moon, blue moon, or other), freeze it in an ice cube tray. Once frozen, pop the ice cubes out, transfer them to a zip-top freezer bag or a tightly closing container, and label them. Place the bag or container in the freezer and take out a cube or two as required.

- Small twigs (including dried herb stems) can be kept on hand to be used when making charms and talismans. They work well inserted into witch ladders, or as the basis for woven spells that ask for crossed sticks as a frame.

- If you feel drawn to making your own cups, dishes, or plates for ritual use, you can start with blocks of clay purchased at an art supply store, and add pinches of soil from specific places in your garden, ground herbs, or dried flower petals as you knead the clay. These additions, along with your intention, can enhance the energy of these very personal magical tools.

BODY CARE

Using herbs in body care has been done for many years. You can follow the previous instructions to make infused oils and then add them to bathwater; try using a light oil such as jojoba or grapeseed for this purpose. An infused oil can also be combined with sea salt to make a body scrub; use 1 part oil to 2 parts salt as a beginning ratio, and adjust to your preferred consistency. For a gentler scrub, you could also use brown sugar.

You could also hang sprigs of fresh herbs in your shower, allowing the warmth of the water to help release the scent and spread the energy.

For bath salts, try grinding your dried herbs into a powder and then stir them into Epsom salt, at a ratio of 4 parts salt to 1 part herbs. For fresh herbs, place roughly chopped plant matter in a cloth tea bag or in the middle of a washcloth with the corners gathered together and fastened with an elastic band, and then add the packet to your bathwater.

DRIED HERBAL BLENDS

Drying herbs and keeping them in carefully labeled jars in a dark place allows you to use them whenever you want to for magic or for cooking throughout the year. You can store the roughly chopped plant matter as you dried it, or you can grind the herbs either by hand with a mortar and pestle, or with a dedicated spice or coffee grinder.

Dried herbs are a quick and easy way to introduce specific magical energy to a particular place that you feel needs it. Keep a selection of tiny bottles or jars on hand so that you can fill them with spoonfuls of your desired herbs and place them where you feel their effect is needed. If you have stone or crystal chips on hand, add one or more that would support your magical goal. If you want to add color to the little spell bottle, add a scrap of paper or fabric of a color that carries associated energy.

Once you've brought in a new harvest of herbs and plants to dry, you can dispose of the old ones with thanks and gratitude. Add them to your compost, or you can burn them as an offering at the spirit house, or at your altar or working space.

Dried herbs can also be used in potpourri, as additions to candle spells (either by rubbing the candle with oil and rolling it in powdered herbs, or by sprinkling the herbs around the candleholder), and in charm bags. One of my favorite things to do with dried herbs is to use them to make sprinkling powders: First, grind your chosen herbs, then put them in a spice-shaker bottle, and shake the herbal powder out in the area(s) that require it. This is analogous to strewing herbs. Leave the powder for as long as you feel it needs to be there to work, then sweep or vacuum it up.

INCENSES AND SMOKE CLEANSING

Burning things releases energy; this is the reason why spells use the method of burning things written on a piece of paper. Burning also releases energy in the form of light and heat created by the fuel. In the case of plant matter, the energies associated with the herbs in your blend are released. For smoke cleansing or offering, sprinkle a pinch or so of your dried plant matter on a lit charcoal disc designed for incense. Make sure to use a heatproof dish filled with sand to hold the charcoal disc. As the smoke rises from the plant matter, waft it with intention around the space with your hand, a fan, or a feather to cleanse the area. If you are burning it as an offering, you may just allow the smoke to rise without wafting it.

Here are some good plants to use in incense blends:

- **Lavender:** A calming herb, lavender is used for health, divination, relaxation, and psychic development. Grind the dried flowers to sprinkle on charcoal or use the stalks with leaves to bundle into a stick shape.
- **Mugwort:** This herb clears energies, leaving a blank slate. It also has a clearing effect on the mind, and a heightening of the extra senses, so it is a good thing to use when starting any working that is going to involve an altered or trance state at some point.
- **Rosemary:** Rosemary is commonly used to protect, ward off negative energy, purify, and bless. Use a fresh spring to dip into water to sprinkle, or grind it and burn it on charcoal.
- **Sage:** White sage is becoming problematic in terms of ethical consumption and cultural appropriation. A perfectly useful alternative is garden sage (*Salvia officinalis*), which grows well in a garden, window box, or as a windowsill herb. Sage is associated with purification and wisdom.
- **Vervain:** Used for protection, purification, and clearing negative energy, vervain is also used for healing and to attract good fortune.

Chapter 9

Practice Witchcraft in the Garden

Magic in Your Garden

Even more magical than working magic with supplies sourced from your garden is working magic in the garden itself. Your garden is your corner of nature, your personal interface with a microcosm of the greater natural world. Designed, built, and cared for by you, it resonates with your energy, and you resonate with the energy the garden produces as well. It only makes sense for you to work magic in that environment.

> Depending on what kind of magic you're performing, you might want to further finesse the phase energy with that of the sign the moon is said to be in. This information is also in Chapter 3.

Whether your garden is inside or outside, you can find a way to work with it magically. Place a cushion in the room where the majority of your houseplants are and sit on it. Lift your cuttings off the windowsill and set them up on your kitchen table. Step out onto your balcony. Lie down in your yard. You can figure it out. Are you bedridden but need garden magic? You can reach out with your own energy and connect with the energy the garden puts out.

TIMING YOUR GARDEN MAGIC

The sun and moon both carry significant power when it comes to the energy of your garden. We looked at planetary hours and the ways the moon's position in the astrological sky map colors its energy in Chapter 3, but there are more ways a witch can draw on the energy of the luminaries.

MOON ENERGY INFORMATION

Lunar energy is one of the key energies used in witchcraft, and green witchcraft is no different. Moon phases are one of the most common methods by which magical work is planned and performed. The general rule is that attraction or growth magic is performed in the first half of the lunar month, when the moon appears to be increasing in the sky. Banishing or magic associated with decrease or reduction is performed in the second half of the cycle, when the moon appears to shrink away in the sky. Review the moon phase energy associations in Chapter 3 to refresh your memory.

THE DAILY SOLAR CYCLE

Timing your magic according to the daily solar cycle can help focus your magic as well. For example:

- **Sunrise** is a time of beginnings. It is an excellent time for setting intentions and launching new projects.
- **Morning** is a time of increasing strength, good for working on creative issues and other areas that require expansion in some way.
- **Noon** is considered midday, but your clock doesn't always accurately reflect the actual point of the cycle. Instead, check the time of sunrise and of sunset, and figure out how many hours of daylight there are. Divide that by two, and you'll have a better idea of when the sun will be at its peak. (This is particularly important if you live in a place where daylight saving time is employed. Moving a clock's setting doesn't change what's happening in the sky.)
- **Afternoon** sees the sun gradually lowering in the sky. It is a time to work on reducing or minimizing things.
- **Sunset** is a good time to address bringing things to completion, putting things away, and closing something's presence or impact.

THE SEASONAL SOLAR CYCLE

The sun also travels on a grander scale, giving us the seasons. The solar energy of one season feels very different from the solar energy of another season. As seen in the moon's cycle, there is a waxing and waning pattern. Here are thoughts on how the seasons influence your magic:

- **Winter energies** are quiet, slow energies. It is a time of hibernation, of recouping energy after exhaustion.
- **Spring energies** are creative, full of potential, and are about planting seeds for future harvesting.
- **Summer energies** are expansive, fertile, and healthy.
- **Fall energies** are about harvest and abundance, and also about preparing to bring the cycle to a close, winding down in preparation for rest.

Drawing Magical Energy from the Garden

Drawing energy directly from your living garden is as simple as drawing energy from the earth when you center and ground. The bonus is that it's energy that you've been cultivating and encouraging.

Let's first take a moment to discuss the differences between living plant energy and energy carried by harvested parts. We touched on this in Chapter 3 very briefly. The best way to learn this difference is to run your own exercise, sensing the energy of some dried plant matter, then sensing the energy of a living plant of the same kind. Compare your notes. What differences do you sense? What similarities? There tends to be a vibrancy to a living plant that overlays its magical energy. It doesn't make it better; it's just different.

Harvesting a plant isn't necessarily cutting its life short. Many plants are grown for the specific reason of being harvested. Beyond that, many plants are single-cycle growers; they're annual plants, destined to die at the end of their cycle, whether that be their own life span or a reality of the turn of the seasons. When we harvest, we thank the plant, recognizing the work and energy that went into growing and its death as part of the natural cycle. In a garden, we support that plant's growth and make sure it has water, good soil, the best growing conditions we can provide for it. We, too, put energy into its growth. And when we harvest it, for magic or otherwise, that energy returns to us in the form of energy to fuel our magic, or energy to fuel our bodies.

Heron Michelle, in her 2018 article "O Tannenbaum: My Witchy Winter Solstice Tree As Fir Magick," does an excellent job of exploring the concept of sacrifice and fair exchange of energy:

Part of the lesson to be found here is that nothing really dies, it merely changes form. Also, the life-cycle transmutes energy in a chain from the sun to the highest order of organism, but nothing escapes their turn to die: everything in the cosmos will rise, thrive, decline, die, to decay, and nourish the next generation who will rise from their compost. This is the same way that every plant and flower we harvest for magick lends their power to our workings, there is a sacrifice, to be sure. But as long as we "fairly take and fairly give," with respect to our plant allies, then this magick can be very potent.

Drawing on living plant energy is simple. It's done in much the same way you'd draw on ambient energy, or the energy of a body of water, or a tree you're sitting under. After centering and grounding, reach out with your personal energy to touch that of the plant. After making contact, ask if you may draw on its energy. Explain that you only need a bit, describe your goal, and wait for the plant's acquiescence before you continue. If there is no response or a negative sensation, thank it for its time and ask a different plant.

Some things to keep in mind when working with plant energy:

- Where the plant is situated is going to influence where you work. If the plant is potted you can probably move it to where you intend to work; if it's a large outdoor plant, you're going to need to work next to its location.
- An offering in thanks to the plant is always important. This is a symbolic exchange of energy. Honor the plant that has worked with you by giving it water, or by giving it a small crystal or other stone that you have washed and purified. A pick-me-up snack of an appropriate fertilizer or soil enricher would also be a nice gesture, but make sure it's the kind the plant or soil needs and that it's the appropriate time of year to fertilize the soil.
- Be very, very careful to not siphon off too much of the plant's energy. This can push it beyond a point where it can recover, and it may die. If it survives, then it may never be the same.

The soil will also be magically empowered with the energy of the plant that grew there. Use this in spellwork to add earth magic tinged with the magical associations of the plant that grew in it.

An alternate idea is to draw the energy of the plant into yourself, then direct it into a receptacle of some kind in order to draw on it at a later date. A stone of similar energy correspondences is one idea; you could also use an image of the plant (drawn or a photo), or a statue or tool that you have prepared. Knot magic is another idea; draw the plant's energy into a rope or cord made of natural fibers, then tie a knot to secure it. Untie the knot later to release the energy.

PLANT FAMILIARS

A familiar is a spirit who aids you or participates with you in spiritual and/or magical work. Familiars are generally thought of as animals, but as a green witch, if you have made contact with the spirit of a plant, and have a personal resonance or connection with one, why not invite it to work with you?

Does the plant spirit need to be associated with a plant you're using in your magic? It depends. Generally, I say no; I believe you can use a familiar of a plant not involved in your spellwork. The reason for this is simple: The plants I resonate with often have energy that can apply to the casting part, not the actual magical goal.

For example, I can call on the purification and strength of rosemary to aid my casting even if my goal is something delicate and relaxing, like making a sleep charm for my daughter. I wouldn't add rosemary to the charm, but I can use its energies to support my own in the execution of the spell.

Seasonal Celebrations in Your Garden

Your garden is the ideal place to celebrate seasonal rituals. Where else can you clearly see and sense the seasonal cycle as reflected in the natural world? Indoors or out, you can honor nature's cycle.

Most of our traditional observances are rooted in agricultural celebrations. The modern Wheel of the Year—eight festivals, each approximately six weeks apart—follows a solar cycle as the seasons turn. Traditional and folk agricultural practices reflect the solar cycle of the year and run on an agricultural cycle that you can usually see reflected in the growth of your garden. Four of these festivals are the solstices and equinoxes, the first day of each of the four seasons:

- Spring Equinox (around March 21)
- Summer Solstice (around June 21)
- Autumnal Equinox (around October 21)
- Winter Solstice (around December 21)

The other four festivals take place halfway between each seasonal marker:

- Imbolc/Candlemas (February 2)
- Beltane/May Day (May 1)
- Lughnasadh/Lammas (August 2)
- Samhain (October 30)

The many traditions associated with the agricultural cycle often have to do with the health of crops, good harvest, and protection of fields and livestock. This gives us a rich source of celebrations that feature gardening as the focus for specific points of the seasonal cycle. These celebrations focus on fertility, strong growth, and successful harvest, intended to bless and protect the crops.

If you live in a place where the seasons aren't as dramatically different as in the upper Northern Hemisphere, think about the changes that do occur. Do different plants flower and fruit at staggered times? Trace out significant things in your location's annual cycle and choose what to celebrate from among them.

Responding to how the seasons manifest and are reflected in your geographic location is more important than adhering to the dates of these festivals. More importantly, weather affects exactly when certain things sprout, bud, and bloom. This is why tracking your garden's annual activity is important, not to mention interesting. Looking back, you can see how a season unfurled and plan accordingly if the upcoming season begins in like fashion.

Autumn may be my favorite season for the quality of light, tree colors, and energies, but spring excites me in a different way. I look forward to seeing the tips of bulb greens make their first cautious appearance in cool soil. I like seeing the red new growth of leaves on the rose bushes. I watch the swelling of buds on the crabapple tree, and the lilac, anticipating their explosions. I remember that the crabapple trees were in full bloom in mid-May of the year I graduated from high school, and I judge how advanced or behind spring is at that time of year by looking at the crabapples in my neighborhood.

Social media has done me a favor in that I tend to post photos of when these things happen, so previous year's memories come up and I can look out the window and see where things are in relation to them. In time, you get a sense of an average time of year when certain events will happen.

SEASONAL RITUALS

If you already celebrate seasonal shifts or festivals, then try moving the location to your garden space, if you don't already use it for that purpose. The physical expression of seasons in your garden can be very supportive of your celebrations. Being surrounded by physical evidence of the season you're celebrating and the associated energies as they manifest in your garden adds an indescribable benefit to your spiritual celebrations.

You may find that how you celebrate changes if you move your celebration to your garden area. That's fine; it just means that your spiritual expression is reflecting the energy of your environment.

If your garden space is large enough you may have to decide where to set up your celebration. If you have a spirit house or a garden shrine, focusing your activity there may feel right. If you have an outdoor altar or magical workspace somewhere in or adjacent to the garden, that may be a comfortable place to perform your rituals. Work wherever you are most comfortable. If your garden is exposed and visible to neighbors or passersby, you may wish to set up a small secluded area that feels more private in which to conduct your seasonal celebrations.

In my previous books I often talk about the difference between creating sacred space and casting a circle to contain magical work and the energy created by it. When celebrating seasonal rituals in your garden space, you're going to have to be the judge of whether just blessing the space you're going to be working in will be enough, or whether you feel that a more robust delineation of your workspace and/or a barrier to outside energies may be needed. To all intents and purposes, your garden is sacred space, to you and to the plant spirits, wildlife, and the garden spirit. Simply recognizing that in a formal statement before you begin may be enough. As always, you are the judge of what you sense in your location, and what you feel you need.

How you celebrate a season or a significant event or change in your garden is absolutely up to you. You can stand in your garden, you can sit on the ground, in a chair, or on a rock; you can lie down on the ground. You can choose the time of day that best reflects the energies you are celebrating or your personal energy needs or expressions. For example, try performing a spring ritual at dawn, welcoming summer at noon, greeting fall at sunset, and hailing winter at night. You can involve the elements or not, as you like. (Candles in jars to keep from being blown out or over can be lovely; incense can be used in a safe holder; bowls of water can be libations for the garden after your ritual; and so forth.) Have food and drink prepared ahead of time and involve it in your celebration, then leave some as an offering for the garden and the garden spirit.

If you usually prefer your rituals to be scripted ahead of time, try to give yourself a minute at some point in the celebration where you ground and center, and speak a blessing from the heart; trust your intuition and do what feels right for the season.

As part of celebrating or welcoming the season, you might want to do something like walking the bounds of your garden area. This allows you to trace the perimeter of your garden space, providing an opportunity to check over the health and status of the edges of your garden's energy, an area that

You may wish to set up intentional energy boundaries to protect your garden around its perimeter. This can help protect the energy of your space, preventing it from leaking away, but more importantly it can defend your garden from negative energies trying to leech its energies away. For ideas about creating energy boundaries and wards and setting up ways to protect a space and attract the sorts of energy you wish it to contain, see my books *Protection Spells* and *The House Witch*.

we might not interact with as often as with the inside sections. You can walk this perimeter with representations of the four elements if you like—a candle in a lantern, incense, a small dish of water and a sprig of herbs to sprinkle blessed water around the perimeter—or just use words, spoken from the heart or a chant repeated to set up positive vibrations as you pass. In this way you keep an eye on the health and strength of the boundaries of your garden and reinforce the magical intention you set for the garden.

PRAYER OF SEASONAL CHANGE

Here's a general prayer that can be spoken at rituals observing seasonal changes:

Help me flow from one state to another
Let me take the best of what the past season brought me,
And carry it forward into the new season.
May I be open to the shifts that seasonal change brings.
May I work with those shifts, and not against them.
Help me understand that the cycle teaches change,
Release, and moving forward.
Help me honor what I leave behind, what no longer serves me.
Guide me as I step forward in the cycle,
As do the trees, flowers, plants, birds, insects, and all life.
For I am one with nature.

You can substitute the word *moon* for *season* if using this prayer while celebrating one of the twelve seasonal moons; see the next section.

THE SEASONAL MOONS

There are a variety of different names for the twelve (sometimes thirteen) full moons of the year, depending on what culture or region you're from. They are generally named for agricultural events or observable natural phenomena.

Before the Julian calendar came into common use, it's likely that the division of time consisted of lunar months. This means that there would have been twelve months of roughly twenty-eight days each. These would have been anchored by the two solstices, the longest day and the longest night.

Choosing a set of twelve lunar month names can be an insightful way to work with your magical garden. Here I list the different names for each moon, drawn from a variety of cultures. Since it's rare that our precise location perfectly mirrors how these natural events are timed, and our personal rhythms or ways of practice also vary, I encourage you to think through these choices and come up with a set that is most appropriate for where you are, both geographically and spiritually. Your associations with the moons should be personal in order for them to be as meaningful as possible. Establishing a set of names for the twelve moons as experienced in your garden will help shape your perception of the year and how the seasonal energies unfold and flow in your life and garden. It's a way of making a personal connection with the events that occur in a larger seasonal context. A three-month season covers many, many changes, after all. Taking time once a month to track the changes reflected in the cycle of nature and the shift in energy that results provides more opportunities to tune your personal energy to that of the shifting seasons. This helps you to keep better track of what changes when and to be more aware of how those changes affect your personal energy.

Names are sometimes repeated from one month to the other in the following lists. Remember, these aren't a science. Different geographic areas that sourced these names could have seen snow at different times.

If picking and choosing among these different cultural names makes you uncomfortable and you prefer to work with an established set of moons from a single source, then take a look at the sets I list in *The Green Witch's Grimoire*. Alternatively, develop your own.

Remember also that while I have these organized as January, February, and so forth, in reality they would be the first full moon, second full moon, and so on. This is another reason for the repetition of names.

- January: Wolf Moon, Ice Moon, Snow Moon, Old Moon
- February: Snow Moon, Hunger Moon, Storm Moon
- March: Worm Moon, Sap Moon, Crow Moon
- April: Hare Moon, Egg Moon, Flower Moon
- May: Flower Moon, Corn Planting Moon, Milk Moon
- June: Strawberry Moon, Rose Moon
- July: Buck Moon, Thunder Moon, Wort Moon, Hay Moon
- August: Green Corn Moon, Grain Moon, Barley Moon
- September: Harvest Moon, Corn Moon, Full Corn Moon
- October: Hunter's Moon, Blood Moon
- November: Frost Moon, Beaver Moon, Oak Moon, Mourning Moon
- December: Cold Moon, Yule Moon, Oak Moon

THE MOONS OF YOUR GARDEN

If none of the names in the previous list have any connection for you, I highly recommend that you develop your own names for the lunar months. This could be a major undertaking; it involves a lot of observation and reflection. It will take a year or more before you can confidently pin down a list. What's more, it's an ongoing process; don't let your list calcify. Evolve it as you feel necessary, but again, don't make sweeping changes before the annual cycle has gone around and you've made your observations again. If, after a few years, you realize that the initial name you decided on doesn't feel right, go through your seasonal notes and rethink. In this time of noticeable climate shifts, stubbornly sticking to a label for a lunar month when it's clearly no longer appropriate makes no sense at all.

Watch how your garden develops over the course of a year. When do the maple leaves bud? When do the crabapple trees bloom? When do the roses drop their petals? When do the robins or geese return? When does the first frost usually happen? Which month sees the most rainfall? (Your local almanac can help with these, as can meteorological records for your location.) You may end up with a list like this, which reflects my area's patterns:

- January: Snow Moon
- February: Cold Moon
- March: Storm Moon
- April: New Leaf Moon
- May: Planting Moon
- June: Rose Moon
- July: Midsummer Moon
- August: Bountiful Moon
- September: Harvest Moon
- October: Apple Moon
- November: Clearing Moon
- December: Yule Moon

It was tempting to name March the Ugly Spring Moon and November the Ugly Fall Moon. Where I live, March here isn't winter anymore, but it's slushy, cloudy, and horribly damp; November is the cold, wet season after the beautiful fall foliage and golden sunny afternoons are a thing of the past. But those names aren't very positive, and we're striving to reflect the movement of seasons by looking at what we do or what is new around us, not what is missing.

In May, we plant our seedlings and seeds for root vegetables like carrots and radishes; it may seem late to many, but we regularly get frosts into early May, and sometimes even later. August is the most productive month; we harvest daily and usually have more vegetables than we know what to do with. September is the autumn equinox, and the moon closest to that is always called the Harvest Moon. October is our main apple-picking month, although where I live we start in early September. In November, we clear out the garden, pulling out the annuals and prepping the perennials for winter. The winter moon names reflect the weather.

SEASONAL PLANNING

As a green witch, working with the seasons is part of your natural practice. You can also assign practical gardening jobs to the turn of the seasons. For example:

- **Fall:** Sharpen and oil your tools before storing them for the winter.
- **Winter:** Review the performance of your garden, plan for the next year.
- **Spring:** Take out your tools and check them over, wiping them down and oiling anything that needs oiling again. (Storage can be surprisingly hard on tools. Even when unused, dirt and dust can build up on them, which can gum up the mechanisms if the tool has them.) Walk around your gardening space and check your planting areas for damage or changes that need to be addressed. Take note of these areas (write them down!), as well as places that will require new topsoil.
- **Summer:** Keep up with the explosion of growth and enjoy!

Casting Spells in Your Garden

Your garden area is a wonderfully creative place for working magic. It's rich in energy, and supportive, as it shares an energy bond with you. I'm not going to outline specific spells you can do; that's not what this book is about. Instead, I'm going to suggest ways you can involve your garden in spell casting and magical work, and ways you can work magic within it.

INTUITIVE AND RESPONSIVE MAGIC

Arranging things in patterns to encourage a specific flow of energy is an interesting way to work magic in the garden. Even just arranging a collection of things in a beautiful shape is a form of garden magic. Think of it as creating magical art that blends various energies to create something new; in fact, I like to think of it as an art spell. Celebrating the beauty of nature in this way is something that we perhaps don't do often enough. Demonstrating that we appreciate the beauty of nature by using it is a form of recognition and gratitude.

Responding to your intuition and allowing it to guide you in creating a garden spell in this manner can be difficult. We're used to visualizing a clear goal in our mind, and choosing herbs or colors to support that goal. Walking into a garden with the intention of responding to the energy of the garden itself and performing a magical act in gratitude for it can be intimidating if you don't do a lot of spontaneous magic. There's a certain poetry to it, however, and it's one of my favorite kinds of magic. Doing what you feel moved to do in response to the energy around you is a wonderful, personal expression of magic.

If there ever was a reason to leave aside your magical tools—if you use them—working in the garden is it. Everything you need is there. Of course, you can bring items out and use them in the garden, if you like, but do try a few workings without anything except what you find in the garden itself. It sparks your creativity and gets you thinking and acting outside your habits.

Look around your garden for things that catch your attention. Fallen leaves, petals, twigs, and stones can all be incorporated into your magic. If you feel the garden is calling you to cut living leaves or flowers off for your magic, follow your intuition. I sometimes call this sort of spell "performance magic," because the creating of it is a process, and part of the magic itself.

Next, begin your magical art. Where are you drawn to create it? What shape are you drawn to use? I use circles and spirals a lot because they feel very organic to me, but there are times when I feel the garden wants a more grounded shape, and then I use triangles or squares.

As you arrange your natural objects, stay open to new ideas or impressions. As the process unfolds, you may feel called to fetch certain other materials from the house to add to the spell. Doing it at this point is fine, because you're responding to the energy, not planning ahead.

Work until you feel the spell is complete. Release the energy connection you maintained while you worked. Allow the art spell to dissipate on its own over time.

IDEAS FOR GARDEN SPELLWORK

Here are some of the ways I have done garden spellwork:

- Candles placed in the earth, surrounded by sticks, leaves, petals, or rocks. Tapers or tea lights work for this. Either way, make sure to use some kind of container for the candles. There are dry roots and fibers mixed in with soil, and they can catch fire or smolder.
- Draw shapes or sigils in the earth using a stick, your finger, or a twig from a woody plant.
- Draw shapes on the ground with cornmeal. This can also be used as an offering.

And there is always the long-term spellwork of placing plants to grow and merge into a certain energy. If you have an indoor garden, you may be able to move the plants into specific formation or arrangements to accomplish something similar on a short-term basis.

EARTH AND WATER SPELLS

There is a time to be precise in witchcraft, and a time to get your hands dirty. There's nothing that brings you closer to the energy of your garden than browsing it for leaves or flowers that call to you and making them into a spell. You can use this spell format for anything you can think of, really, but I find it works best for the kind of magic that doesn't require precise, specific change.

If I'm looking for magic that draws general, intuitive change, then this is the kind of spell I use. Complicated, finicky magical goals are not suited to this kind of technique.

These are the kinds of spells that my daughter and her friends love to do best. You can do it one of two ways: Start with some water in a bowl and add the components, then stir; or make a dry version by beginning with a handful of soil.

You'll Need:

- Leaves, petals, rocks collected from the garden (see following steps)
- Cup of water or cup of soil
- Bowl, dish, or bucket
- Chopstick or twig
- Optional: Spell components from indoors (berry for sweetness, touch of honey, and so on)

What to Do:

1. Make sure you have a clear idea of your magical goal.
2. Before you start, collect petals, leaves, and stones from your garden.
3. For a water-based potion, begin by pouring the cup of water into the bowl. For an earth-based potion, begin with the cup of soil.
4. Add the leaves and petals and/or stones from the garden, stirring with the chopstick or twig, and concentrate on empowering the mixture with your magical intent.
5. If you're making a water-based potion, add a few sprinkles of the soil. If you're making a soil-based potion, add a few drops of water.
6. If you brought supplies from inside, add them when it feels appropriate.
7. Keep stirring and visualizing. When you feel it's ready, carry the bowl to where it feels right to be.
8. You can leave the bowl in the garden or pour it out to spread the magic that way.

WINTER MAGIC

Don't overlook winter as a season in which to work magic in your garden. There is plenty that you can do when there is snow on the ground. For example:

- Gather snow from specific places in your garden and melt it indoors for holy water blessed by the energy of the area in which you collected it. If you can identify the plant, shrub, or tree and shake or brush the snow off it into a bowl, the resulting water will carry aspects of the energy carried by the plant.
- Use snow from the garden and sprinkle mixtures of dried herbs, leaves, or flowers on top. As it melts, it will turn into a potion.
- Keep the snow in a resealable container in your freezer, and scoop some out when you need it to add garden energy.
- Snow water is great for purification and blessing. If you're working a spell that will initiate slow change, snow water is a great addition.

Snow is important to a garden. It's critical for groundwater levels, and for insulating perennial plants. It also helps rehabilitate the soil.

Using Your Garden for Meditation

Your garden is a refuge and place of spiritual connection. Making it a place for meditation is an excellent use of that space and that energy.

Meditation is an ideal way to communicate with the spirit of the garden. Keeping track of your contact with it and the messages you receive (in either your garden journal or a meditation log) means that you can track how the spirit shifts as your garden develops and evolves. How does it change from year to year?

Your garden is a place of support and nurturing. When you need comfort, surrounding yourself with that energy and allowing it to flow through you can be calming, healing, and nourishing. Reach out to the magic you've cultivated; it's an ideal place to calm the spirit and look within, seeking calm, balance, and harmony.

Like working magic or celebrating seasonal shifts, meditation can be done anywhere you feel comfortable in the garden. The spirit house, the garden shrine, or your altar workspace are all places to try meditation. Do you discern differences between your experiences when meditation is performed in these different locations? Is there a particular spot in your garden where you feel more serene, more at peace than anywhere else? That would be an ideal meditation spot.

As for timing, do garden meditation when you feel unsettled or jittery, unfocused or agitated. If you want to schedule regular meditation, try doing it during the hour of the Moon; the energy of that planetary hour is a good default.

Your goal is to listen. Calm your thoughts; ground and center your energy; lean on the energy of the earth to help replenish low energy levels, or use it to sink extra personal energy to help balance the level of your energy.

Being active with nature is important, but it's equally important to stop and to listen to what it has to tell you. We are busy people. Our minds are constantly buzzing with activity every moment we are awake. Allow yourself to pause for a time, and open yourself to revive your spirit and refresh your essence.

The goal of meditation isn't always to communicate. Sometimes, it's just to be, to exist. It can feel awkward to sit down with the goal of doing literally nothing, to be passive. But in garden meditation, it's sort of an active passivity; you're allowing the energy of the garden to flow around and through you, communicating without active effort. It may sound a little contradictory, and rather like you're trying to juggle two opposing goals, but it's the type of thing that can be better sensed than explained.

Sometimes the point of meditation is to have an exchange of information, to communicate with the energy around you for information.

Once you've grounded, centered, and cleared your mind, and feel balanced, open your heart and listen to what the energy of the space has to say. Receive any messages that it has for you. These can come in the form of inspiration, emotion, or new thoughts arising in your mind. This kind of meditation can be used to attune yourself to your garden's needs, or to reach out to the wildlife in it.

In Conclusion

YOUR GARDEN SHOULD BE A PLACE of spiritual nourishment. Even the work and maintenance can be a spiritual undertaking, allowing you to focus on the physical activity without judgment. Consider the concept that Zen labor teaches, that work is practice; physical activity that nourishes the self and others is honorable. By keeping your attention on the physical task at hand, by being in the moment, we connect with the energy of daily life. A meditative practice like caring for a garden brings you into contact with something outside yourself. Responding to the needs of the garden allows you to be open and insightful, in touch with your physical care for it.

The garden, and our care and reverence for it, is like a microcosm of our connection with nature at large. Nature is our home, our environment in which we live and thrive. Separation from it leads to both sides being the poorer. Your garden is a hands-on gateway to participating in the cycle of nature and benefiting from the insights it will bring you. Every year will be different, and that's part of the magic. No spring will ever be the same as a previous spring, and that is right and good. Like relationships with people, your experience with a season will be different from year to year.

Stand in the midst of your garden, your magical space, and ask yourself: What brings you joy this time?

Bibliography

"16.2A: Soil Composition." Retrieved 7 September 2021 from https://bio.libretexts .org/Bookshelves/Microbiology/Book%3A_ Microbiology_(Boundless)/16%3A_Microbial_ Ecology/16.2%3A_Soil_and_Plant_ Microbiology/16.2A%3A_Soil_Composition

Alden, Temperance. *Year of the Witch: Connecting with the Seasons Through Intuitive Magic.* Newburyport, MA: Weiser Books, 2020.

Barth, Brian. "How to Grow and Harvest Grains in Your Backyard." Retrieved 7 January 2021 from https://modernfarmer .com/2015/08/how-to-grow-and-harvest-grains-in-your-backyard/

Bartlett, Sarah. *Knot Magic: A Handbook of Powerful Spells Using Witches' Ladders and Other Magical Knots.* London, UK: New Burlington Press, 2019.

Beaty, Vanessa. "15 Organic DIY Garden Fertilizer Recipes That'll Beautify Your Garden." Retrieved 23 July 2020 from www.diyncrafts.com/22484/home/ gardening/15-organic-diy-garden-fertilizer-recipes-thatll-beautify-garden

Bertelsen, Karen. "How to Grow & Harvest Wheat on a Small Scale." Retrieved 9 January 2021 from www .theartofdoingstuff.com/im-growing-wheat-this-year-and-you-can-too/

Cowan, Eliot. *Plant Spirit Medicine.* Newberg, OR: Swan Raven & Co., 1995.

Daniels, Estelle. *Astrologickal Magick.* York Beach, ME: Weiser, 1995.

David Suzuki Foundation. "How to Create a Pollinator-Friendly Garden." Retrieved 18 January 2021 from https://davidsuzuki.org/ queen-of-green/create-pollinator-friendly-garden-birds-bees-butterflies/

Debret, Chelsea. "How to Build a Regenerative Garden at Home." Retrieved 4 December 2020 from www.onegreenplanet .org/lifestyle/build-regenerative-garden/

"Gardening by the Moon: Learn How to Garden by the Moon's Phases." Retrieved 19 January 2021 from www.almanac.com/ content/planting-by-the-moon/

Grant, Amy. "Homegrown Oat Grains—Learn to Grow Oats at Home for Food." Retrieved 8 January 2021 from www.gardeningknowhow.com/edible/grains/oats/homegrown-oat-grains.htm

Hanson, Dave. "Growing Cinnamon in Pots." Retrieved 17 December 2020 from https://sagegarden.ca/blogs/the-sage-garden-lab/17049368-growing-cinnamon-in-pots

Joffe, Daron, and Susan Puckett. *Citizen Farmers: The Biodynamic Way to Grow Healthy Food, Build Thriving Communities, and Give Back to the Earth*. New York: Stewart Tabori & Chang, 2014.

Larum, Darcy. "Moon Garden Design: Learn How to Plant a Moon Garden." Retrieved 17 July 2021 from www.gardeningknowhow.com/special/spaces/moon-garden-design.htm/

Michelle, Heron. "O Tannenbaum: My Witchy Winter Solstice Tree As Fir Magick." Retrieved 7 December 2020 from www.patheos.com/blogs/witchonfire/2018/12/o-tannenbaum-my-witchy-solstice-tree-as-fir-magick/

M.G., Leslie. "Spawning a Mycelial Mélange: How to Grow Mushrooms Outdoors." Retrieved 18 December 2020 from https://gardenerspath.com/plants/vegetables/grow-mushrooms/

Penry, Tylluan. *Knot Magic*. Tonypandy, Wales, UK: Wolfenhowle Press, 2014.

Rost, Wiebke. "Plants and Planets." Retrieved 17 July 2021 from https://pflanzenkunst.wordpress.com/2018/07/13/plants-and-planets/

Schwartz, Judith D. "Soil As Carbon Storehouse: New Weapon in Climate Fight?" Originally published March 4, 2014. Retrieved 3 April 2021 from https://e360.yale.edu/features/soil_as_carbon_storehouse_new_weapon_in_climate_fight

Simms, Maria Kay. *A Time for Magick*. Woodbury, MN: Llewellyn, 2001.

"What Is a Makerspace?" Retrieved 6 January 2021 from www.makerspaces.com/what-is-a-makerspace/

Hardiness Zones

HARDINESS ZONES ARE SYSTEMS OF classification that use the meteorological data of a geographic location to determine what plants can successfully grow there. This data includes minimum temperatures, rainfall and snowfall, humidity, and so on. Other factors will impact your choices, such as soil type, microclimates (escarpments or bodies of water can affect weather patterns within a larger hardiness zone, for example), and how long the minimum temperature season lasts, among other things. Hardiness zone is a good way of narrowing down your potential choices, but you'll always need to do research to find out what plants are viable in your precise location. Sometimes that research involves trying to grow something and failing. Everything is a learning experience, and every experience with a plant is a way to access and participate in the shifting energies of the life cycle practiced by nature.

There is no single method used worldwide to define hardiness zones. Various continents use climate description, minimum and maximum temperatures, and other factors to establish their definitions. Check to see if your country has a web page (most likely in the agricultural section of the governmental site) that focuses on growing zones. Some allow you to enter your location and access a list of plants observed in the area, enabling you to choose from among a list already adjusted for your zone.

Note: Climate change is affecting hardiness zones. Older printed resources may differ from the current information available. Check the dates of online resources as well, to help you stay up to date.

The following is a list of links to maps of plant hardiness zones in various countries and continents around the world:

- United States: https://planthardiness.ars.usda.gov
- Canada: www.planthardiness.gc.ca/?m=1
- South America: www.backyardgardener.com/garden-forum-education/hardiness-zones/sazone/
- Europe: www.houzz.com/europeZoneFinder
- Australia: www.anbg.gov.au/gardens/research/hort.research/zones.html
- New Zealand: https://liddlewonder.nz/zones.php
- Africa: www.backyardgardener.com/garden-forum-education/hardiness-zones/africa-hardiness-zone-map
- Asia: https://commons.wikimedia.org/wiki/File:Asia_Köppen_Map.png
- China: www.backyardgardener.com/garden-forum-education/hardiness-zones/china-hardiness-zone-map

Index

Air plants, 72–73

Altars, 171

Alternative gardens, 26–28

Angelica (*Angelica archangelica*), 122

Aquatic/aquarium plants, 68–69

Arbors, 172

Aspidistra (*Aspidistra elatior*), 63

Astrological gardens, 43–49
 about: overview of, 43–44
 astrological signs and ruling planets, 48
 planetary hours and, 45–47
 planets and their attributes/energies and plant associations, 44
 timing gardens with astrology, 45–49

Basil (*Ocimum basilicum*), 122

Bay (*Laurus nobilis*), 123

Bead charms, 156

Beltane (May Day), 200

Blessing gardens, 93–94, 158–62

Body care, 190–91

Branches/twigs, for spellwork, 189, 190

Cacti, 71–72

Calendula (*Calendula officinalis*), 109

Caraway (*Carum carvi*), 123

Carnation (*Dianthus spp.*), 109

Casa Blanca oriental lily (*Lilium orientalis 'Casa Blanca'*), 54

Celebrations in garden, seasonal, 199–206

Centering and grounding, 15

Chamomile (*Chamaemelum nobile, Matricaria chamomilla*), 110

Charm bags, 155

Chives (*Allium schoenoprasum*), 124

Cinnamon (*Cinnamomum spp.*), 121, 124

Cleansing garden space, 91–93

Comfrey (*Symphytum officinale*), 129

Community gardens, 26–27

Community-supported agriculture, 28

Compost(ing), 18, 19, 23, 24, 160

Container gardening, 79–81

Cover crops and grains, 24, 144–48

Daffodil (*Narcissus spp.*), 110

Daisy (*Leucanthemum vulgare, Chrysanthemum leucanthemum*), 111

Decor to enhance garden, 56, 170–72

Deities associated with gardens, 162–63. *See also* Spirits

Design, choosing, 95–96

Dill (*Anethum graveolens*), 125

Divination, with garden, 183–85

Easter Lily Cactus (*Echinopsis oxygona*), 54

Eco-awareness, 21–23

Elemental gardens, 57–59

Elements, garden and, 17

Energy, access to, 42–43

Energy, drawing from garden, 196–99
Equinoxes, 199, 206
Evening primrose (*Oenothera biennis, Oenothera pallida*), 54

Farmer's Almanac (*Old Farmer's Almanac*), 164–65
Ferns, 63
Fertilizing, 25, 198
Field spirits, 163–64
Flax, 147–48
Flowering tobacco (*Nicotiana spp.*), 54
Flowers, 107–20. *See also specific flowers*
    about: color meanings, 107–8; common ones to grow, 108–20; edible, 37; native species, 39
    to enjoy at night, 53–56
Food and cooking, garden for, 35–37. *See also* Fruit; Recipes; Vegetables
Four o'clocks (*Mirabilis jalapa*), 54
Foxglove (*Digitalis purpurea*), 130
Fruit, 134–35, 174–76
Fungi and mushrooms, 142–44

Gardenia (*Gardenia spp.*), 54, 111
Garden(ing). *See also* Gardens, green witch types; Goals and planning garden; Magic
    about: attitude toward, 214; using this book for, 10

advantages of having, 12–14
alternative gardens, 26–28
building connection to nature, 16
eco-awareness and, 21–23
four elements and, 17
journal, 18, 96–98, 101
for meditation, 211–13
modifying existing garden, 34–35
most powerful magic, 10 (*See also* Magic)
plant spirits and, 19–21
recognizing natural life cycle and, 16–19
regenerative gardening, 23–25
as spiritual reflection of you, 14–16
why you need for your craft, 12–14
Gardens, green witch types. *See also* Indoor gardening and houseplants; Magic; Outdoor gardens
    about: basic components, 42–43; energy access and, 42–43
    astrological gardens, 43–49
    elemental gardens, 57–59
    food/cooking gardens, 35–37
    magical elements gardens, 37–38
    moon gardens, 49–56 (*See also* Moon)
    solar gardens, 57
Gates, 172
Genius loci (spirit of place), 153–54
Geranium (*Pelargonium spp.*), 112

Goals and planning garden, 30–40
    about: envisioning, designing your garden, 30–31
    basic components of green witch garden, 42–43
    budget considerations, 30
    choosing planting cycle and design, 95–96
    garden for food and cooking, 35–37
    garden for magical elements, 37–38
    hardiness zones and, 32
    magical oasis garden, 38–39
    modifying existing garden, 34–35
    planning for next year's garden, 104
    planning stages (magical and practical), 31–34
    rewilding, 40
    seasonal planning, 207
    soil and, 33
    weather and, 33–34
Ground cover, 148. *See also* Cover crops and grains
Grounding and centering, 15
Grounding energy, 65, 136, 146, 181
Guerrilla gardening, 27–28

Hardiness zones, 32
Herbs, 121–33. *See also specific herbs*
    about: for body care, 190–91; common culinary, 122–29; common non-culinary, 129–33; dried blends, 191; freezing in oil, 178–79; growing cinnamon, 121;

growing cuttings from scraps, 76; harvesting, storing, prepping for use, 176; incenses and smoke cleansing, 192; making wreaths with, 186–87; native species, 39; possibilities to grow, 36; recipes with, 177–80 (*See also* Recipes)
creating records for herbal entries, 100–103
source for interpreting uses of, 166–68
strewing, to break up negative energy, 92
surprise (uninvited) plants, 165–68
Hours, planetary, 45–47
Houseplants. *See* Indoor gardening and houseplants
Hyacinth (*Muscari racemosum, Hyacinthus non-scriptus*), 112

Imbolc/Candlemas, 200
Indoor gardening and houseplants, 62–73. *See also* Blessing gardens; Cleansing garden space; Container gardening
air plants, 72–73
aquatic plants, 68–69
cacti, 71–72
common houseplants, 62–65
growing racks, 66
multiple mini garden areas, 66–67
succulents, 70–71
terrariums, 67–68
windowsill and window box gardens, 76–79
winter gardening, 74

Infused oils, 188–89
Intuitive divination, 183–84
Iris (*Iris florentina*), 113
Ivy, 63–64

Jam, making magical, 174–75
Jasmine (*Jasminium spp.*), 113
Journal(ing), 18, 96–103, 168
Jupiter, hour of, 47

Lady's mantle (*Alchemilla vulgaris*), 130
Lavender (*Lavandula spp.*), 114, 192
Lawns, rewilding, 40
Lilac (*Syringa vulgaris*), 114
Lily (*Lilium spp.*), 54, 115
Lily of the valley (*Convallaria magalis*), 115
Lughnasadh/Lammas, 200
Lupine (*Lupinus spp.*), 116

Magic. *See also* Gardens, green witch types; Spirits
about: overview of magic in garden, 194; this book and, 9
amplifying magic of ingredients, 169
casting spells in garden, 207–9
charm for welcoming new plants, 152–53
charms for tools/equipment, 150–51
decor to enhance garden, 170–72
drawing energy from garden, 196–99
earth and water spells, 209–10

garden care tips, 164–68
garden folklore and traditions, 163–64
for garden protection and health, 152–62
genius loci (spirit of place), 153–54
for health of garden (blessings and wassailing), 158–62
offerings, 154–55
techniques for garden magic, 155–57
timing garden magic, 194–96
using grown items in witchcraft, 186–92
Magical elements, garden for growing, 37–38
Magical oasis garden, 38–39
Mars, hour of, 47
Meditation, using garden for, 211–13
Mercury, hour of, 47
Mint (*Mentha spp.*), 125
Moon
decor for moon garden, 56
gardening by, 165
gardens, 49–56
garden to enjoy at night, 53–56
hour of, 47
phase garden, 50–53
phases and associated energies, 49, 52–53
plants associated with, 50
seasonal moons, 203–6
timing garden magic and, 194–95
transit of, 47–48
void of course, 48–49
Moonflower (*Ipomoea alba*), 55

Mugwort (*Artemisia vulgaris*), 131, 192

Mullein (*Verbascum thapsus*), 131

Mushrooms and fungi, 142–44

Nature. *See also Farmer's Almanac*
  building connection to, 16
  hands-on with natural cycle, 42
  recognizing natural life cycle, 16–19

Night, garden to enjoy at, 53–56. *See also* Moon

Night-blooming jasmine (*Cestrum nocturnum*), 55

Night phlox (*Zaluzianskya capensis*), 55

Norfolk Island pine (*Araucaria heterophylla*), 64

Nutmeg (*Myristica fragrans*), 126

Oasis garden, magical, 38–39

Oats and oatstraw (*Avena sativa*), 146–47

Offerings, 154–55

Oils, infused, 188–89

Oracle decks, 184–85

Orchids, 73

Outdoor gardens, 81–82. *See also* Blessing gardens; Cleansing garden space; Container gardening

Pansy (*Viola tricolor*), 116

Parsley (*Petroselinum crispum*), 126

Philodendron (*Philodendron spp.*), 64

Planetary gardening. *See* Astrological gardens

Planning garden. *See* Goals and planning garden

Plants. *See also* Cover crops and grains; Flowers; Fruit; Herbs; Indoor gardening and houseplants; Mushrooms and fungi; *specific plants*; Trees; Vegetables
  about: overview of indoor and outdoor gardens, 62
  to enjoy at night, 53–56
  planting what you like, 106–7
  surprise (uninvited), 165–68
  talking to, 21

Plant spirits, working with, 19–21

Pollinators, 22, 39, 40, 94, 117, 131

Poppy (*Papaver rhoeas*), 117

Pothos (*Epipremnum aureum*), 65

Pressing samples, 98–99

Primrose (*Primula vulgaris*), 117

Racks, growing, 66

Rain lily (*Zephyranthes drummondii*), 55

Recipes
  about: making jam magically, 174–75
  Boquet Garni, 178
  Freezing Herbs in Oil, 178–79
  Herbal Butter, 177
  Herbal Salt, 177–78
  Mirepox, 181
  Mulling Spices, 181

Savory Shortbread, 179–80
  Vegetable Soup, 182–83

Regenerative gardening, 23–25

Rewilding, 40

Rocks, painted, 156

Rose (*Rosa spp.*), 118

Rosemary (*Rosmarinus officinalis*), 127, 192

Sage (*Salvia spp.*), 127, 192

Samhain, 18–19, 200

Samples, pressing, 98–99

Saturn, hour of, 46

Schefflera (*Schefflera spp.*), 65

Scraps/waste, growing vegetables from, 26, 74–76

Seasonal celebrations/rituals in garden, 199–206

Seasonal planning, 207

Seasons, blessings for garden, 159–60

Shrines, 171

Sleep blessing, 161

Snapdragon (*Antirrhinum majus*), 118

Soil
  eco-awareness and, 21–23
  exposure, limiting, 24
  quality/composition, planning garden and, 33
  wassailing fertility ritual, 161–62
  zero tilling, 25

Solar cycle, timing magic and, 195–96

Solar gardens, 57

Solstices, 18–19, 199

Spells. *See* Magic

Spider plant (*Chlorophytum comosum*), 65

Spirit houses, 171

Spirit of place (*genius loci*), 153–54

Spirits
deities and, associated with gardens, 162–63
field, in different cultures, 163–64
plant, working with, 19–21
plant familiars, 198–99

Spiritual reflection, garden as, 14–16

Sprout magic, windowsill, 78

Statuary, 172

Succulents, 70–71

Sun, hour of, 47

Sunflower (*Helianthus spp.*), 119

Tarragon (*Artemisia dracunculus*), 128

Terrariums, 67–68

Thyme (*Thymus vulgaris*), 128

Tools and equipment, gardening, 84–90
about: overview of common gardening tools, 84–88; witchy tools, 88–89

charms for, 150–51
connecting to, spoken spell for, 150
dedicating, 89–90
magical tools, 189–90
releasing, cutting ties with, 150–51

Trees, 138–42

Tuberose (*Polianthes tuberos*), 55

Tulip (*Tulipa spp.*), 119

Valerian (*Valeriana officinalis*), 132

Vegetables, 135–38
about: to consider growing, 36; recipes with (*See* Recipes)
bulb, 75
leafy head, 75
magical associations, 136
root, 75–76
from scraps/waste, 26, 74–76
what and how to grow, 137–38

Venus, hour of, 47

Verbena (*Verbena officinalis, Verbena spp.*), 129

Vervain (*Verbena officinalis*), 132, 192

Violet (*Viola odorata*), 119

Void of course moon, 48–49

Wands, making, 186, 189

Wassailing, 161–62

Water(ing)
blessing water used for watering, 156–57
botanical waters, 187–88
rainwater for spellwork, 189–90

Weather, 33–34, 164–65

Wheat, 147

Windowsill and window box gardens, 76–79

Winter gardening, 74

Winter magic, 211

Witch bottles, 155–56

Wormwood (*Artemisia absinthium*), 133

Wreaths, herbal, 186–87

Yarrow (*Achillea millefolium*), 133

Yucca (*Yucca spp.*), 55

Zero tilling, 25

MORE FROM BESTSELLING AUTHOR
ARIN MURPHY-HISCOCK

PICK UP OR DOWNLOAD YOUR COPIES TODAY!